PERSONAL EFFECTIVENESS

PERSONAL EFFECTIVENESS
A Strategy for SUCCESS

by George S. Odiorne

MBO, Inc., Westfield, Massachusetts

Cover and book design by The Headlineship, Chicago.
Typefaces: Cover–Compacta Bold
Text–Antique Olive & Avant Garde Gothic

Copyright © 1979 by George S. Odiorne
Published by MBO, Inc., 157 Pontoosic Road, Westfield, Mass. 01085.
All rights reserved. No part of this book may be reproduced by any means, transmitted, or translated into a machine language without written permission from the publisher.

ISBN: 0-9602950-0-3
Library of Congress Catalog Card Number: 79-88613
Printed in the United States of America

Contents

Preface v
Part I: Introduction 1
1. The meaning of effectiveness 3
**Part II: Preparing yourself as a person
who makes things happen** 11
2. Communication—the exchange of meaning 13
3. Your reading skills can be improved 18
4. The sharpening of your memory and how it helps you 26
5. Constructing a self-image 33
Part III: Moving things, people and situations 39
6. Understanding the activity trap and how to avoid it 41
7. Understanding other people
   to get things and people going your way 47
8. The importance of clear goals 51
9. Getting things done 58
10. Styles of leadership 63
11. Situational management 69
12. Using your time effectively 74
13. Simplifying the job—working smarter, not harder 83
14. Organizing other people's work
    to make them help you more 89
Part IV: Activating others 95
15. Three keys to activating other people to go your way 97
16. Three steps to motivation 103
17. Face-to-face communication makes things happen 108
18. Using transactional analysis
    to make your transactions pay off 114
19. Working effectively through small groups 120
20. Being effective before a crowd 128
21. Planning follow-up development 132

Preface

Some people get more done than others.

The manager of the local hamburger stand probably doesn't work shorter hours or any less hard than the Secretary of Defense. The manager of the small country inn works just as hard as the manager of the Waldorf Astoria in New York. But there are some pretty sizable differences in what each accomplishes in a day.

The people who make things happen aren't really all that different from the people who never get off the dime. They have the same two arms and legs and often the same metabolisms. The difference then lies in what goes on in their heads. People who make things happen are better organized, target their efforts better, and generate more results than the other people.

Making things happen is mainly in your mind.

That is why a book like this one can help you get more out of your time, you life, and your effort.

Some people shrug off the idea that they can make more happen in life. "I just don't have the energy to work like some of those people," they protest. And this points up another interesting fact: The kind of people who make things happen generate more energy than people who don't get things done.

It is apparent that certain kinds of work create more than enough energy to get the work done. Other kinds of work seem to drain us even before we start doing it. Just thinking about certain tasks is enough to produce fatigue. That most boring task you do causes you to start out exhausted before you even begin. Yet a creative and innovative job (such as playing a key part in a play or building a community task force to stamp out corruption in city hall) can gin up all the energy you require to accomplish the task.

The conclusion from all of this is that energy isn't like a gas tank. It's not something you fill up, perhaps by a good night's sleep and a hot breakfast, but that then runs dry as time goes by. Energy is created by your approach to life and to work. But there is more to getting things done than tackling them with great gusto and zest. What's important is organizing your approach to problems, being ready for action before the action starts, developing some skills that make work easy, and especially getting other people to go in your direction. This book should change your behavior, and make you more effective in getting wherever it is you want to go.

George S. Odiorne
Amherst, Mass. 1979

Part I
Introduction

Matching theory and action is a relatively untouched area of concern in human relations. Scholars and theorists like to deal in concepts and philosophies. Functioning and practical people are often so busy doing things that they haven't time to think about what they are doing. . much less write out the essence of action. This book is aimed at capturing the essence of action, and especially at noting what you do, do differently, or stop doing when you are making things happen.

Chapter 1
The Meaning of Effectiveness

One of the meanest, most despised stereotypes of our time is that of the efficiency expert. That's the person who snoops around watching people as they work, then telling them—and their boss—how they are goofing off. The efficiency expert hides behind file cabinets spying on ordinary workers finding out their most intimate secrets at work, how they relax here and take a coffee break there. The efficiency expert then tries to speed everything up, to get people to work faster, and to eliminate all of the wasted moments in a work day until the workers are turned into machines. Small wonder we don't like them!

> Efficiency experts don't have a thing to do with effectiveness, and this book is opposed to the whole idea of efficiency experts. Being effective means working smarter, not harder.

- Lots of people work very hard and kill themselves doing things they shouldn't have been doing in the first place.
- Some people pride themselves on their efficiency, but when they get to the end of their lives and look back they discover they were in the wrong game on the wrong field and it was all futile.

Twenty Eight Keys to Personal Effectiveness

In this book you'll find summarized the results of many years of research by a host of behavioral scientists, industrial engineers, learning theorists, systems experts and researchers. The aim is to make you personally effective. Since footnotes and the rest of the apparatus of scholarly research would slow you up in reading the book—and becoming more effective—these have been dispensed with. If you want to get into that, for example if you want to write a book of your own or read more books on the subjects covered, there is a list of such readings at the end of this book in Part IV. Meanwhile, lets's examine twenty eight key guides to personal effectiveness—your strategy for success. Each will be expanded upon in the rest of the text, but first I'll list and briefly explain each one.

☐ **(1) All human beings are success seeking animals.**
John Baptiste Lamarck, the famous natural scientist of the past century, arrived at four conclusions about the process of evolution and change as it governs the lives of people and animals. We all have a drive for perfection, we all adapt our behavior when we discover we aren't on track, we are all capable of making quantum leaps and major changes in direction and our futures are all governed to some extent by our pasts, Lamarck said. Psychologist T. A. Ryan said that our behavior is mainly intentional behavior; that is, it intends to go somewhere. Without such a realization we may drift and waver in our behavior, which is a perfect definition of ineffectiveness. We shilly-shally about, drift to and fro, waffle and fritter away our time and our lives. Fortunate indeed are the people who learn early in life what their purposes are, for they create a personal vision of success for themselves.

☐ **(2) Life is most fully lived when it has meaning, intention and goals.**
It is wasted and futile when there are no goals and intentions. The attractions of monetary pleasure, of dissolution and ignoble ease are more delusion than reality. The lasting pleasures are those of anticipation and realization, things that humans can find and which animals are often denied. The first step toward effectiveness then is finding meaning and converting it into explicit aims and targets.

☐ **(3) You can't possibly be successful unless you define what success consists of before you set out to achieve it.**
You never reach your destination unless you know where you want to go, or unless you have some pretty clear idea as to what sort of place it is that you are seeking so that you can recognize it when you get there. This means that to be effective you have got to get a firm grip on your objectives for if you don't know where you are going any road will get you there.

☐ **(4) Your goals are a function of who you are and what you want to become as well as any outside or external targets you might be shooting at.**
You think you want to become rich; and accordingly if I were to ask you to name your life's goals or what success would consist of you might respond by naming a sum of money, like a million dollars or some other figure. Yet that is merely symbolic of your real values. You are telling me what you are, what values you have, what ideals your ego is seeking. This goal is only symbolic; the real goal is to actualize and realize what you want to be. **You cannot really be successful without a clear self-image.**

☐ **(5) Success always involves other people in some way or other.**
Perhaps you picked up your image or goals from watching others and try to imitate them. You don't merely want to become rich, you would like to be "as rich as Rockfeller" or you'd like to "keep up with the Joneses." More than we might like, our goals require that we be in touch with others. We pick up our goals from others. People with whom we compete prevent us from achieving our goals. And it is only in contact and collaboration with others that we can get where we want to go.

☐ **(6) Your chances of success are greatest if you are in tune with the world around you and your chances of failure are greatest when you get out of touch with that world.**
We are social animals, for the most part, and only hermits and misfits want to get wholly away for all time. Of course we all like to be left alone occasionally, but the people who want to get away from the world and live on an island like Robinson Crusoe simply won't make it in this world. They have to create a world of their own where the competition and pressures which thwart their aspirations are eliminated. The only competition and barriers then are those presented by nature and their own inadequacies. On the other hand, there is nobody there to help them get where they want to

go. Neither is there anybody around to recognize, applaud and praise their achievements, and this takes a lot out of them. **You need other people to be successful.**

☐ **(7) Your sanity and your success both depend upon being authentic.**
You cannot be effective if you are a faker. You cannot operate with two or three of life's spark plugs unscrewed to make a phoney impression on somebody. You need to follow three of life's cardinal rules in order to keep from going nuts, or at least slightly neurotic (which means out of gear):
    (a) You must **know** yourself.
    (b) You must **like** yourself.
    (c) You must **be** yourself.
People who live lives of affectation and sham, disguise and concealment find tension and unease too great to really get on with the great challenges and crusades which confront successful people. They are like the centipede that gets tangled up in its own hundred legs trying to figure out how it works.

☐ **(8) You need to have a sound memory for your own past and that of society.**
If you don't know where you are and something about how you got there you are doomed to repeat every mistake you've ever made. This means you must concentrate upon some of the retention skills of memorizing and keeping things stored up where they will be available to you for future use. Most people can improve their memories and learn to manipulate information from their own experience. Contrary to the old folklore, experience is not always the best teacher, but it is an essential member of your faculties which you can't ignore if you are to be personally effective.

☐ **(9) Your senses can be more fully developed to improve your effectiveness and assure your success.**
Those people who are the most successful are often those with the best cultivated powers of observation. They have all of their receptors in fine tune, and learn from those incoming messages. It's been said that President John Kennedy could read five times as fast as the average college graduate while retaining more of what he read. He was also a sharp listener. President Jimmy Carter's most highly developed personal skill–far better than his public speaking, as many have noted–is his ability to listen closely and clearly to others and to understand what they have said. Understanding others when they speak or write may be his greatest personal skill.

☐ **(10) Effective people don't get enmeshed in the Activity Trap.**
The least effective people are those who become so involved in activity they lose sight of the reasons for the activity and that activity becomes an end in itself. It's true that the most effective people are active, but their activity is directed toward goals which are never lost sight of, and that activity which doesn't contribute to those firmly fixed objectives is abandoned or reduced.

☐ **(11) The clarity of your goals is the most important element in shaping your personal effectiveness.**
If you don't have goals—or if they are murky, muddy or unclear—your effectiveness will be greatly reduced. If you have conflicting or mutually exclusive goals they will get in each other's way and stop you from reaching either. As an old Nigerian folk saying goes, "the man who tries to catch two rats at once will catch neither." Or as Air Force General Edward Rawlings once said, "if you aim for nothing that is exactly what you'll hit."

☐ **(12) The ultimate test of your effectiveness is making things happen.**
There are some people who make things happen, other people who watch what goes on and respond to it, and an even larger number of people who don't even know what is happening. It is the first category which comprises effectiveness. Being attentive to one's goals—and making things happen toward achieving those goals—is the distinguishing characteristic of effective people. Neither style, nor caste, nor character, nor background, nor personality define the difference between the effective and the ineffective person. Effective people are best distinguished from the ineffective by the answer to the question: "Did they get the job done?"

☐ **(13) Time is of the essence in effectiveness.**
As has been noted, mortality is a characteristic feature of the human race. Thus how time is used is equal in importance to having clear goals in determining your effectiveness as a person. Those people who get more bang for their daily allocation of hours and who have developed some practical time stretching skills are more effective than people who waste the most precious commodity mortals have—their time. Like the Old Testament book of Ecclesiastes, Gail Sheehey dramatized the importance of the passing of time and the accomplishments with each of the stages through which we pass in her book **Passages.** Wasting time is wasting life.

☐ **(14) Effectiveness means managing situations even more than it means managing yourself and your life.**
You are but one element in your situation. To try to affect changes and improvements in your life may require that you react to situations and, even more importantly, that you change the situation in which you find yourself. This means managing and interacting with your environment, the people you contact, and the natural and social elements in that environment.

☐ **(15) Effective people do things simply, without a lot of complexity.**
Professors, scholars and pedants who spend their time complicating life and knowledge often make the world and the people in it less effective. On the other hand, people who make us more effective are those who simplify our lives. To be effective you need to uncomplicate your life.

☐ **(16) Effective people use other people and in turn are used by them without deception, but in honest acknowledgement of their mutual dependence on one another.**
The most effective people are those who know not only their own powers and abilities, but also their limitations and weaknesses. For those weaknesses and inadequacies they are comfortable relying upon others who have compensating strengths. They organize others, delegate to them powers to act on their behalf, and use the pooled strength of others to help them get where they wish to go. Only the weak and defensive adhere to the admonition, "I'd rather do it myself, mother."

☐ **(17) There are three basic ways to activate other people that you need to use artfully.**
The first is to compel others to do things by ordering them about and by punishing them if they don't obey (or by making some use of power to make them wish they had complied). This produces counter-responses and revolt in may instances. The second method of activating others is to persuade, sell and conjole them to go in your direction. The third way to get other people to be active on your behalf is to consult with them, to find out what they want and to strike coalitions which advance the purposes of all parties. This consultative manner of activating others produces the highest level of permanent effectiveness but is the most difficult to learn and to apply.

☐ **(18) If you would understand others, look inside yourself.**
Emerson suggested that you "look in your own heart if you would understand mankind." The motives and aspirations of others are the keys to finding areas of joint concern and possible lines of collaboration. The wants of others can be explained in external stimuli, in the consequences of past behavior, and in the internal drives and yearnings which are common to us all. Much of the behavior of others is adaptive to those drives and how they respond to the barriers that life and its discontents throw in their paths. Understanding human behavior is an essential ingredient in being effective in the world of people.

☐ **(19) Three major elements comprise the motivational factors that impel us to move.**
The first influence is information. People are motivated to move by pure raw information. This is especially true of information about what is expected, where help comes from, how much freedom we really enjoy, how we are doing, and what the rewards will be. The second element in motivation for effectiveness is obstacle removal. We need to know how to react and adapt to life's obstacles. The same obstacles that stop one person apparently don't bother another. The third element is using payoffs creatively. We reward people or withhold rewards, and in turn we are rewarded and have rewards withheld for different behaviors. Learning what pays off and what doesn't is part of your effectiveness planning.

☐ **(20) Face-to-face communication with others is the best form of interaction.**
People who would make things happen will find that their skills in dealing with others one-on-one is the major vehicle for putting things on the right track. We can only resolve life's disputes, or strike bargains with others, or change the behavior of others through such face-to-face encounters. When things are done impersonally, perhaps by means of a written memorandum, they are not accomplished so quickly or as surely as when they are done with personal contact. The effective person is likely to be adept at handling face-to-face contacts well.

☐ **(21) For transactions to be effective, it is necessary that people communicate on an adult level.**
Research shows that all of us have at least three different ego states in which we live. We behave like parents, like children, or like adults at varying times. When we make transactions like a parent communicating with a child, or like children with one another, our effectiveness is diminished. The most effective level of transaction is that in which we treat others like adults and in which we act as adults ourselves.

☐ **(22) The major social fabric of life is the small group.**
We're most likely to be effective in getting the best out of ourselves and others when we work in small groups. Most effective family groups, social clubs, teams, classes and departments are comprised of small groups. The nature of small groups and their management is a primary skill of the effective person. Inability to understand and work with small groups will hamper your personal effectiveness.

☐ **(23) Large crowds, mobs and rabbles are more apt to be governed by emotion than by reason.**
Where getting things done requires persuasion or a change of behavior by large clusters of people, appeals to emotion will be more successful than appeals to reason and rationality. Thus the mass media and public speakers have proven to be most effective when they've played upon the instincts, hopes and fears of their audiences. This can be used for good or evil, for ennobling or debasing purposes. It is the approach of cultists, crusaders, politicians and advertisers.

☐ **(24) Effective people are life-long learners; ineffective people stop learning early.**
Effectiveness in your personal life and the attainment of success is neither an action nor a condition; it's a process of **becoming**. When we stop growing we are dying... or we're dead. As Andrew Carnegie said: "Everything is perfect, it is getting better." The emerging person is the effective person. The key question for the effective person is not "When do I arrive?" but "How do I do even better?"

☐ **(25) You cannot learn to be successful in a single course or book.**
If you were to believe the advertisements that come in your mail and those you see in magazines and on TV, success can be achieved by getting rid of your erroneous zones, taking sensitivity training, enrolling in est, meditating, becoming assertive, studying transactional analysis, jogging, or getting tuned in to your biorhythms. If any of these remedies worked none of the others would be around. That should tell you something: There is no easy answer to finding success and being effective. As Willard Gaylin has said, "Life is very complicated. You can't find happiness by following some simple recipes." Becoming effective is hard work. It is true that some people work hard and fail, but also there are those who have proper goals and who have targeted the path to success but fail because they didn't work at it. Hard work is one of the essential elements of personal effectiveness.

☐ **(26) The place to start in making yourself more effective is where you are right now.**
Many people make all of their self-development plans contingent upon one impossible condition, such as "when the kids are grown," "as soon as my mother is better," "after I get another raise," or "when I hit the state lottery is the time I'll start applying my new strategy." An alternative to this is to lament the **if-onlies** of life: "If only my older brother hadn't gotten the favorite spot in the family business" or "If only I had not been trapped into an early marriage." The place to start with a planned strategy for effectiveness greater than you now have is where you are today. Study yourself. Look at the risks and opportunities in your present situation. Analyze your own strengths and weaknesses. Then start improving from there.

☐ **(27) You'll do better in an improvement plan if you make some commitments to other people to start improving.**
As we all know, losing weight is easier if you make a hefty bet with somebody that you will lose more than he or she. Similarly, you're more likely to stick with your improvement plans if you've joined a club and have to stand before others and state your goals, and then admit your failures. . . or get cheered for your successes. If you develop a strategy for being more effective and successful you will probably last longer at it if you take somebody along with you on the journey. Making commitments–and keeping them–is an essential element in defining effectiveness.

☐ **(28) There are no free lunches, so everything you achieve will cost you something.**
One of the great barriers to effectiveness is that we want everything but don't want to pay for all of it. To develop the skills of the athlete means giving up certain pleasures (such as loafing, eating and drinking), and taking up training and practice. For the most part, the price paid by executives in getting to the top is measured in hours of work and study, and in deferred gratification. If you don't want to pay the price, you don't really want the goal. We always live in a world of trade-offs and compromises. Whatever you truly set your heart on will surely be yours. . . if you pay the price.

Rate Yourself

These twenty-eight points are a summary of what you will read about in some detail in this book. They aren't a precise outline of the table of contents, but they are the underlying precepts which are expounded, explained and demonstrated in this book. Taken together, they constitute a strategy for achieving personal success by being personally effective.

As you read, you probably noted a box before each of the twenty-eight points. Go back through this chapter now and place an X in the boxes before those items you feel you are strong on, those you feel you **do not** need help in. If you feel that you do need to make some improvement in a particular area to become an even more effective person, leave that box empty.

After you have looked each of the twenty eight points over and checked off those areas in which you feel you are already personally effective, add up the number of boxes checked to rate yourself according to your overall level of personal effectiveness.

If your score is 25-28 points, you are effective in your own eyes and you see your own life as being successful at this time. Congratulations! You are a model for us all.

If your score is 20-24 points, you are successful and effective in your own mind and need improvement in but a few areas for sharpening your personal effectiveness. This is a very good score.

If your score is 15-19 points, you are effective in some areas but have room for improvement in many others. You should start mapping your personal effectiveness strategy now and then keep it up. Your overall personal effectiveness score is fair.

If your score is less than 15 points, you are probably plagued by some major areas of uncertainty and ineffectiveness. But not all is hopeless. By mastering the strategies for personal success and effectiveness you can be better in the future than you are now.

Good luck...

Part II
Preparing Yourself as a Person Who Makes Things Happen

The keen interest people have in action, motion, efficiency and relevancy in their behavior was never more apparent than it is today. College campuses are more quiet at the end of the 1970s than they were at the start of the decade as students concentrate on learning to pursue careers "where the action is," where they can make things happen.

The key ingredients of making things happen, of making the place where you sit and walk the place where the action is, are what I'm talking about in the following pages. Starting with how you communicate—your knowledge, your memory and your self-image—we move on to the action in the words we speak to others, in the roles we play in life's drama, in the conquest of oppostiion, in the persuasion of others, and in lives of productive contacts with other humans.

Chapter 2
Communication–The Exchange of Meaning

Communication is being in touch with other people. You might quickly conclude that this means talking, or perhaps writing. It's far more than this.

Communication includes all of your behavior which results in an exchange of meaning. It includes everything you do which transmits intentions or ideas to another person, or by which another person transmits ideas and intentions to you.

- It could be making a speech at the PTA.
- It could be reading a book or your daily newspaper.
- It might be listening to your spouse or to a speech on TV.
- It could be making a presentation to the board.
- It might be a gesture, a snort, a sneer, a scowl, or a nod of approval.

Communication is closely tied to stirring up what you have received in your memory drum and spinning it out later.

Running the entire gamut of behavior, communication is hard to manage. You'll do it better if you have a **system.** That's what this book is all about.

You and the Human Condition

More than two billion people cover this planet. They live, work, raise families, exploit minerals, sail the seas, and probe the hemisphere and beyond. Being part of the human race, we must relate to the environment. If we are to be leaders, we must make things happen in one tiny segment of the world. This means that we can keep from falling off the roster of the human race.

Wars erupt periodically among these humans. Organizations split into squabbling groups, companies fail, families break up, and racial strife develops at various times and places. The big issues of our times are those of human relationships. Scientific progress doesn't seem to assure growth and happiness for the human race. What is the cause of these undesirable conditions? It's that people aren't in touch with one another. Misunderstanding, failure to persuade, quick conflict, lack of unity in groups and nations, and open warfare are the consequences of the failure to communicate.

Closer to where we live, people operate at less than their full potential as humans. They live in half awareness; they live lives of monotony, fear, or anxiety because they aren't in complete vibrant control of themselves and their environment. Their senses are limited, and the extensions which other people make of themselves into new and self-fulfilling activity aren't realized.

Economic Man

Adam Smith, the philosopher-economist who is generally credited with being the father of capitalism (at least of the theory of modern capitalism), made an interesting assumption. He stated that the cause of the wealth of nations was "the invisible hand" which operated without the need for central control by government. It was the market place where each person, carrying his or her own "private interests and passions," communicates with others of similar aims. The result is a self-regulatory kind of competition which leads to a higher standard of living for all.

Although he wrote this in 1766, and his theories are now accepted only in vastly modified form, Smith pointed up the importance of a mechanism for communication if we are to prosper economically.

While the Western world lives now in a kind of administered capitalism, the importance of communication in the market place is greater than it was in the day of Adam Smith. A message to another continent that took months in Smith's day now flashes around the world in seconds. For Smith to have travelled to London from his home post in Glasgow where he taught moral philosophy would have been a major undertaking requiring several weeks to complete. Today, by jet, a professor can fly from Glasgow's Prestwick airport to London's Heathrow airport in seventy minutes, and then on to New York City's John F. Kennedy airport in three hours and forty-five minutes aboard the Concorde. Cutting across time zones at a speed greater than that of sound, he moves so swiftly that his body's metabolic clock reels at the unsettling collapse of time and distance.

The problems of communication have not been alleviated by this constriction of time, however. On the contrary, our apparent improvements have left us closer to the brink of destruction, and the problems of economics–how people make a living–haven't changed very much in the world at large, aside from the West, since Smith's time. Starvation, plagues, wars, and other disasters seem to have accelerated their pace in much of the world.

For the person who works for a living the problems of communication seem greater than they ever were. Large organizations take on the apparent characteristics of dinosaurs, often too large to draw sustenance from their environment. Conflicting groups fail to reach understanding in matters of labor-management relations. Inside firms there are products which are invented but not brought to market in time to meet competition. Errors, failures, and people working at less than full potential are all too common. In the world of creative chemistry, of mass transport, or electronics and space technology, communication is not an incidental process. It is a natural resource which we haven't studied, explored and developed adequately. Marshall McLuhan, the Canadian scholar, declares that "our human senses, of which all media are extensions, are also fixed charges on our personal energies. These media shape the awareness and experience of each one of us."

We face our inadequate skills in communication daily. As radio, TV, the telephone, and printed media expand our senses, they emphasize our shortcomings as communicators.

The Model for Direct Action Communication

I have used a model in shaping the strategy for developing personal effectiveness which attends this book. A model is simply a working framework around which the specific sessions and ideas are draped. The model used is one that's been developed by the informational theorists. These are the scientists who have studied communication at

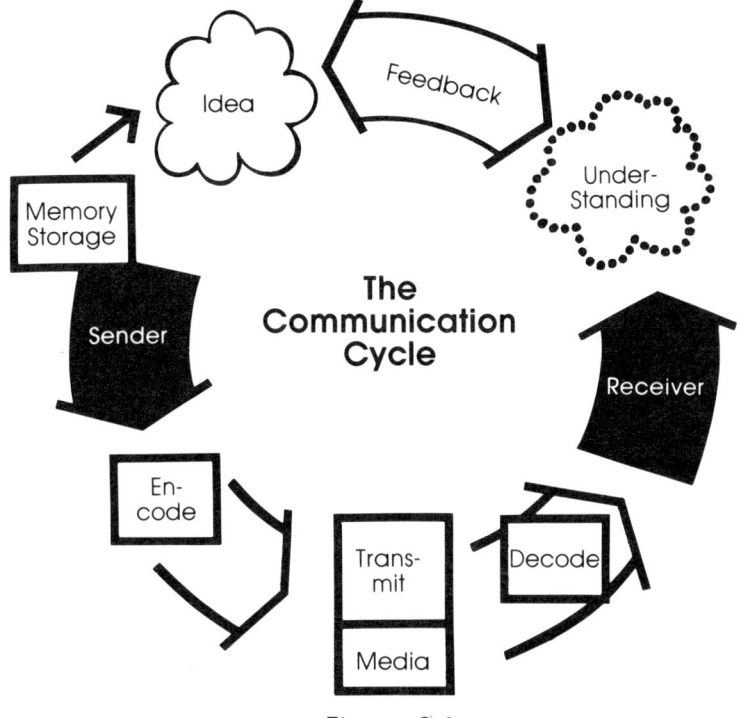

Figure 2-1

the deepest scientific levels. When they communicate with one another about communication they use mathematics. Since we're more concerned with day-to-day communication in the market place, I'll skip the formulae, but the model remains.

Figure 2-1 depicts what the model looks like as it will affect you. The model is really an analogue of communication in its basic process. In telephone and electronic communication, or in the disciplinary process as applied by a supervisor, the process is much the same. When a scientist makes a presentation to a sponsor, when a salesperson makes a sales pitch, or when a group of managers enter a conference room to solve a problem or make a policy, the model is at work. Here's how it works:

- A **sender** is a person who initiates a message. This is a person who has something to say, or is someone who has an idea or intention that he or she wishes to place in the mind of a **receiver,** or in the minds of several receivers. What the person hopes to achieve is understanding of the idea and, consequently, perhaps a change in the receiver's behavior. We say the sender wants to persuade the receiver.

- The **message** is an idea which exists in the mind of the sender. It's pretty obvious that before a person can communicate he or she had better have an idea. If that idea isn't clear, it should be clarified inside the sender's head before he or she **transmits** it to others. If the sender doesn't understand the message, there is little chance that the receiver will understand it either.

- Information is stored in the memory of the sender which must be pulled out in coherent form. Often people "forget," which means they don't have a set of memories to manipulate. Note this about so-called intelligence: Without a memory drum stocked with information you have nothing to manipulate. Sharpening your ability to memorize–especially your ability to remember faces, names and people–is essential in dealing with problems in human relations. (What you can do to improve your memory will be covered in detail in Chapter 4.)

- When we convert our ideas into words in our own minds we use a **code.** The code may consist of words or numbers that are either written out or spoken. Occasionally we use other symbols as well, but usually we think in words and numbers. Skill in transforming our ideas into words and numbers is not some academic exercise. We choose the code which fits the receiver. When talking to a child we may use small words; when talking to a technical expert in our field we probably use some jargon that is unique to that specialty. The trick in coding a message is to put it into that code which the listener or reader must use in decoding it. Suppose we don't? Then the message will go right past the receiver's decoding equipment and won't reach that person's mind at all. The result is no communication, no exchange of meaning, no understanding, and no change in the other person's behavior.

Being an Effective Receiver

Not all of the responsibility for communication lies with the sender. The receiver, too, has an obligation to develop his or her decoding equipment and to use it effectively. There may be skills of listening which you can develop. You may enlarge your own vocabulary. Your emotional barriers to listening can be recognized and allowances can be made for them. The mechanical techniques of receiving, collecting, classifying, sorting and comparing information received can be sharpened through desire and practice.

Emotional and psychological filters may be applied, often unconsciously, to messages that come to us. These filters can be controlled to increase our effectiveness in human relationships.

Communication efficiency decreases drastically when the receiver and the sender fail to check back with each other to see how well understanding has been achieved. This takes us into dialogue, interviews, conferences and questioning. The failure to achieve dialogue is at the root of so many human relations that the list could be endless. Marital, industrial, educational and mental health problems would be substantially reduced if more dialogue could take place at a gut level.

The Importance of Feedback

Feedback completes the communications cycle. It is the basis of information theory and rounds out the model with which I'll be dealing in some detail in this book.

How do we summarize this matter of feedback? As a general guide in organizational settings, two major means are required to make communication work. They are the dialogue and the memo.

Dialogue means simply talking to another person.

A memo is written communication. There are three major types of situations in which the cold memo will not work and where it will probably do more harm than good:

1. You can't solve a conflict with a memo.
2. You can't strike a bargain with a memo.
3. You can't change another person's behavior with a memo if that behavior is at all deeply rooted.

Of course, if the information being transmitted is routine, a memo might do; "The office will be closed on Christmas Day," doesn't need a discussion. But if you want to resolve a conflict, strike a bargain or change any deeply rooted behavior you will have to employ dialogue because it involves feedback.

A memo confirms in writing what has been agreed during the dialogue. If a bargain has been made, it should be put on paper and sent to the other party. If a conflict is solved, the new conditions should be described in writing and sent to the other party. If changes have been agreed upon, summarize the agreement in writing. It can be a good point of reference later. The faintest ink is stronger than the best memory.

Chapter 3
Your Reading Skills Can Be Improved

One of the most common complaints of most of us is that we lack the time to handle the many details of our daily workload. In the search for ways in which you can improve your personal effectiveness, one suggestion is to decrease the amount of paperwork that demands your attention. Another way of putting it is to suggest you reduce the reading demands on your time. This could, of course, be accomplished by delegating to an assistant the bulk of memoranda, policy statements, proposals and whatnot that find their way to your desk. In practice, however, this cannot always be done. The professional will be quick to point out that all of that reading is necessary and that we cannot escape responsibilities to our employer by depending on another's interpretation of important facts. This leaves us with the alternative of reducing our own reading time per unit of material.

By the time we've reached adulthood our reading skill has become so much a part of us that we tend to think of it as virtually automatic, unchanging and unchangeable. We also assume that we are about as efficient a reader as others of similar interests and academic achievement.

An engineer had from time to time been struck with what he considered to be his wife's rather casual, hasty and superficial approach to printed matter. At least this was how he characterized her reading to me. Both he and his wife were detective story devotees and on occasion they read together from the same book. The engineer noted that his wife was usually ready to turn the page when he was only halfway through. This was mildly irritating to him but since it was "only a detective story" he allowed that her cursory superficiality did not make a great deal of difference. He prided himself on his meticulous approach to the printed page which he felt yielded him optimum comprehension. However, in a study of reading methods and an objective analysis of his reading efficiency, he was quite surprised to find that he was a rather slow, ineffective reader compared to other adults and that his wife was able to read nearly twice as fast as he with equal comprehension. He learned that speed and accuracy are not, as many like to think, self-exclusive. Studies of comprehension under conditions of increased speed have shown that, in general, overall comprehension increases because more reading ground is covered in the allotted time. Comprehension per page or per paragraph remains about the same in the case of the average, conscientious adult reader.

Reading Habits of Successful People

Many years ago the Harvard Business Review circulated a questionnaire to twenty thousand subscribers. Responses revealed that two newspapers were read by almost all of the business executives who took part in the study. About half of them read the Wall Street Journal and about a third read the New York Times; three-fourths of them read one or more trade publications, such as Iron Age or Women's Wear Daily. The most widely read books were in the areas of personnel psychology, business management, economics, marketing and accounting.

Estimates of the amount of time the average executive spends reading per week have been the objective of several surveys. An unpublished study by George William England indicated that technical executives read on the average about four hours per week. Other studies show that the average executive spends about fifteen to twenty hours per week reading at the desk at work, including correspondence, memoranda, technical reports and trade journals. Furthermore, most executives are afflicted with what has been called "briefcaseitis"–carrying work about for study on the commuting train or at home. They are likely to do a considerable amount of miscellaneous informational and recreational reading in addition to their work-connected reading. It is not unusual for an executive–or a person on the way up–to read a total of twenty hours or more a week. This adds up to a thousand hours or more of outside reading per year.

More conservatively, let us suppose that the average career person in business or government reads ten hours per week, or five hundred hours per year. If this reading time could be cut in half without loss in comprehension, two hundred and fifty hours of valuable living time could be saved every year.

Differences Between Readers

Individual differences in reading effectiveness are greater than we may think.

In a study conducted in a manufacturing plant in Detroit a random selection of one hundred foremen were given the Michigan Speed of Reading Test. This test measures the number of paragraphs read and understood in a given length of time.

The range for the group of foremen was from seventy paragraphs to only four paragraphs. The fastest reader of the group read almost eighteen times as much in the same length of time as the slowest!

Eight per cent of the group were found to be below the sixth-grade level for reading ability; twenty-two per cent were below the eighth-grade level. On the other hand, nine per cent were found to read at or above the level of the average college graduate. One foreman with only eleven years of formal schooling was found to have a reading speed superior to that of the average college senior.

How Much Improvement?

The amount of improvement in reading skills that can be expected from training, including self-training, is considerable. One reason for this is that reading is not an innate (or inborn) natural skill. Reading is learned. And often it has been learned incorrectly. Further, after an elementary school level of competence is reached, reading is an ability that does not necessarily improve as more of it is done.

Yet, it is important to know, reading can be greatly, even dramatically, improved. The average adult participating in a course in effective reading can increase his or her rate by one hundred per cent without difficulty, and without loss of comprehension. That buys you a bundle of time!

A question that might be asked by the thoughtful reader is, "How much is left of these dramatic increases in reading speed after a period of time?" A University of Chicago group of trainees retained about eighty-five per cent of their gain after six months. A group of twelve faculty members at Air Technical School retested six months after completion of a reading training course retained ninety per cent of their gain. In the case of a group of more than a hundred students who made a conscious effort to maintain skill, they read at an average rate ten per cent above that achieved at the end of their seventeen-hour course. The conclusion is that skills learned can be fairly well retained; self-training can possibly increase them further.

A reading improvement course is a good investment in your own effectiveness.

How To Speed Up Your Reading

The initial approach to more effective reading is realizing its feasibility. Research results demonstrate the usefulness of treating in reading methods. **Faith in these facts and in your ability to improve are the first steps.**

Once the resolution to increase your reading power has taken hold, the next step is its implementation. A course with a competent instructor and appropriate materials and devices, such as objective tests, manuals and mechanical pacing devices like the Science Research Associates Reading Accelerator or Harvard Reading Films, would be ideal.

In the absence of such accoutrements, self-training is a reasonable undertaking. This will require a little more effort and self-discipline, however. Motivation may be greater under the competition of participating in a group with a common goal. Still, you may set up your own goals and compete against yourself during the period of self-training. Your work will be simplified if you provide yourself with a good manual. A number of those are available.

There are six areas you need to cover in your self-administered reading improvement program:

(1) **Getting started.** Informal but sufficiently accurate estimates of your present efficiency level in reading may be made with materials in your library, a watch with a sweep-second hand, and a patient confederate. Select an easy work of fiction (such as a detective story) and a more difficult piece of writing (such as an article in a technical journal). Determine the average number of words per page for each. Then, in turn, do a five-minute stint in each of the two types of printed materials, reading at your normal, comfortable rate and marking your starting and stopping place. At the conclusion of each exercise be prepared to answer questions on the material put to you by your assistant. This comprehension check is important because if you do not know what you have read, you simply have not been reading in any effective sense. Divide by five (minutes) the number of words read, and you will have your rate for two kinds of material. The easy fiction should be read at about three hundred fifty words per minute, the difficult technical material at about two hundred fifty words per minute.

An important point here is that the rate for the two kinds of reading matter should differ. If this is not the case, you may be a word-for-word reader whose approach to the printed symbol is rigid and unselective. Engineers, accountants and other technically trained executives often have difficulty shifting gears and persist in the habit of giving close attention to each printed symbol whether it appears in a highly technical research report or in a newspaper or a detective story. The truly skillful reader more or less unconsciously shifts his or her reading rate for maximum efficiency in grasping the ideas presented by reading an article in the Daily News at more than five hundred words per minute and one the the Harvard Business Review at three hundred words per minute.

(2) **Mechanics of the reading process.** In order to better understand the differences between good and poor readers it is useful to study the mechanics of the reading process. For example, eye movements in reading are peculiar in that reading takes place only when the eyes are at rest. Along a line of print the eyes move in jumps or jerks from left to right. The stopping places where the eyes record the printed words (and pass signals on along the optic nerve to the brain) are called fixation points. You can observe and count the actual eye movements in reading by placing a small mirror on the page of a book opposite the one you are reading; a person looking over your shoulder can see the stops and starts of your eyes as reading is going on. A more elegant, accurate device for recording eye movements is the ophthalmograph which provides a beam of light that falls on the cornea of the eye. As the subject reads a selection, a moving photographic film record yields information on the rate of reading and the number of fixations and regressions per line as well as the speed and accuracy with which the eyes sweep back and adjust to a new line of print.

As might be guessed, the eye movement record of a highly efficient reader is characterized by relatively few fixations per line–the eyes take in a number of words at each stop–and practically no regressions. A reader who continually goes back and rereads a word or phrase cannot be expected to read at a satisfactory rate.

You will want to check yourself to be sure that your span of apprehension is large enough, that is to say that you are not stopping for each word but are taking in groups of words and phrases at each fixation point. If you are a habitual regressor, attempt to push forward without rereading, even though at times you may be sure that you have missed something important. Surprisingly enough, if you push yourself, in time you will find your eye-brain team cooperating to give you the sense of the material the first time around.

A related but somewhat different mechanical aspect of reading is what is known as vocalization. When traveling in a plane or bus where you can surreptitiously watch other passengers, concentrate your attention on the readers. You may be rewarded by finding several who, though they may not actually be reading aloud, are moving their lips while reading. Not so obvious but almost as handicapped is the vocalizer who although not forming words with his or her lips, is reacting to them with parts of the throat. Movements or vibrations should be quite evident to you. The reason that vocalizing is such an enemy of speed is that the eye-brain team is more effective in producing meaning when it is not called upon to key its efforts to the slower reacting muscles of the vocal apparatus. Because much of our early reading instruction is oral, many adults retain inappropriate and cumbersome oral reading habits which have no place in efficient communication via the printed page.

(3) **Self-training hints.** Now, with a knowledge of the mechanical aspects of reading as well as an estimate of your own skill, you are ready to commit yourself to the practice that leads to improvement.

If you have acquired a manual you will find study objectives laid out for you in a meaningful fashion. Charts, self-rating devices and comprehension checks are used to measure progress. However, if it is your intention to use materials at hand for practice, you might be wise to make up a rate chart like that in Figure 3-1. On the vertical axis place "number of words per minute"; on the horizontal indicate the test period or date. A rate check may be made about once a week, with regular practice in between checks. The rate may be plotted on the chart as a graph. Select at least two types of reading material for your self-tests: easy fiction or nonfiction (such as Reader's Digest which is at about eighth-grade level) and more difficult and possibly job-related articles or books. Keep the same "test" materials throughout your training period so that the difficulty level will remain practically constant from check to check. This will save you from estimating words per page each time. Materials for practice may be anything that is interesting to you. For optimal results practice should be undertaken regularly. Provide yourself with a comfortable well-lighted spot away from distracttions. In the early weeks of self-training select fast-moving, intriguing material. Consciously force yourself to read at a rate faster than usual. Attempt to read in meaningful phrases or thought units rather than word for word. "Go through the door," for example, is easily handled in one fixation by a skillful reader. Make a mental note of any tendency to

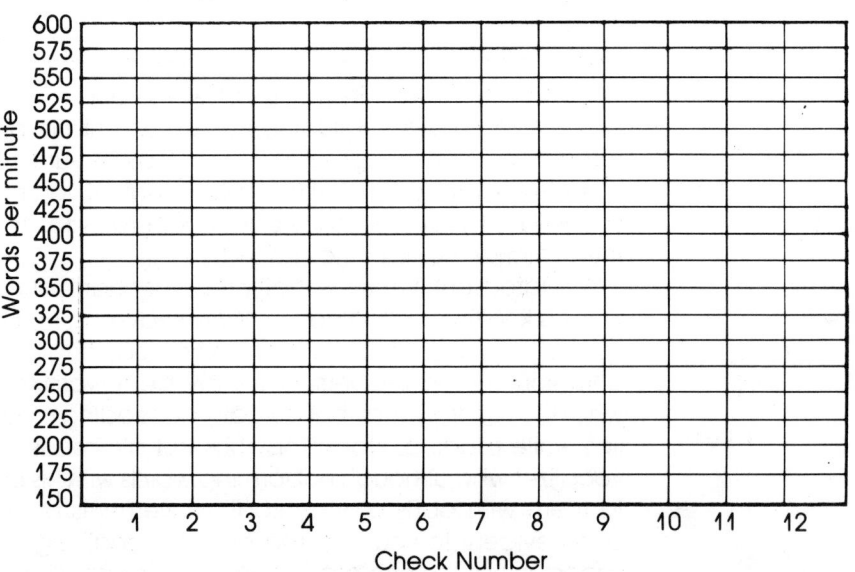

Figure 3-1

regress and try simultaneously to suppress this. A helpful aid here is the daily newspaper. Competence in reading phrases can be increased by preparing a 3x5 card with a slot in it the size of a line of newsprint. Slip the card down a news column and try to read the whole line in one rapid fixation.

(4) **Problem areas.** Special problems may arise as you are pursuing your goal of increased efficiency in reading. Some of these that deserve mention are difficulties in concentrating and remembering, vocabulary deficiencies, and slow or incomplete comprehension. Obviously, these overlap.

For example, take the sentence, "The Martins found the climate in the Bahamas particularly enervating." If you understand this to mean the weather was generally invigorating and productive of a sense of lively well-being, you will be missing the point not only of this sentence but possibly of an entire paragraph. A vocabulary weakness is contributing to poor comprehension.

Another example is that of the lawyer who reads a dissertation for physicists on the mathematical assumptions underlying a particular reaction. The lawyer will not only experience comprehension difficulties but will also be unable to remember little of what is read. In this case the background of experience is the limiting factor.

The printed page is not, of course, the same for everyone, and we should not attempt to set impossible tasks for ourselves. The physicist would, in all probability, be equally at sea in trying to unravel some of the finer points of a legal document.

However, even within the framework of a realistic reading task, some individuals have difficulty in concentrating. Perhaps the most common cause for this is failure to provide a good setting for thoughtful reading. A busy office–with bells ringing, doors swinging and a multitude of other minor interruptions–does not help the reader to concentrate. Similarly, the jolly living room–equipped with TV jiggle shows and well-nourished off-spring–does not make for an ideal setting for acquiring maximum meaning from the printed page.

Habits of a lifetime may militate against efforts to concentrate effectively. The reader who has become accustomed to using printed material instead of, or in addition to, a sleeping pill and does the bulk of his or her reading comfortably cradled in bed may be the one who complains most loudly about concentration difficulty. Over a period of years reading has come to be associated with a relaxed, semisomnolent state of mind and the mere act of reading may induce this state even at inappropriate times when the reader is not in bed!

A degree in self-discipline will be necessary in your practice sessions. When you find your mind wandering, either toward a dreamy, sleepy state or to things unconnected with the particular subject matter before you, blow the whistle on yourself. Stop reading, walk around a bit, get a drink of water (or perhaps a snack), then return to your practice session with a stern self-reminder that you have another half-hour's work to do. Check yourself after five minutes or so to make certain that you are remembering adequately what you have read.

Authors have thoughtfully provided the reader with a variety of aids to comprehension. The title of a chapter will often be helpful in guiding the reader's thinking. It may produce a train of thought that will aid comprehension. What goes through your mind when, in a book on investment counseling, you read a chapter headed "Gaining Profits by Taking Losses"? You will be reading with a purpose and will take advantage of information given you by the author. Some of the questions that have occurred to you may be: How can this be? What kinds of losses are referred to here? When should I take a loss? Then, as you read the chapter, you find ideas falling into place and you find new ideas emerging as the pieces of a puzzle come together–in short, as comprehension is achieved.

In addition to chapter headings, other cues to reader thought and eventual comprehension are found in subheads that appear in different type from the main body of material, in topic sentences that may be the first or second sentence of a paragraph, and in graphs, tables and maps which serve to summarize and clarify a mass of material. You will look for signpost words to help you understand what the author is saying, for example, "first," "on the other hand" and "to summarize."

Above all else, comprehension is most readily achieved if you are active as you read. The continuous asking of questions, sifting of ideas and summarizing of important points are marks of the effective reader. In some instances you may want to carry activity a step farther by taking notes, making an outline, or checking portions of the material for future reference. Your method, as well as the rate at which you read, will depend upon your purpose.

(5) **Skimming.** The most rapid reading of all–skimming–has sometimes been summarily dismissed as not real reading. The agile skimmer may cover two thousand words or more per minute. It is obvious that such a person does not read every word or even every sentence, yet he or she is selectively skimming off the cream–either getting the gist of the piece or looking for particular information.

Much of the material, perhaps two-thirds of it, that piles up in a day on the desk of a busy executive can be disposed of by skimming. Success in this art depends to a great extent upon developed skill. After you have gained confidence in your ability to increase your rate without comprehension loss, you will find you are relying on key words to assist you. You must force yourself to rely even more heavily on key words to become an efficient skimmer. Concurrently with the use of key words, you will be noting central thoughts, guiding yourself by signpost words, and rapidly sifting important ideas as they present themselves.

A mark of the successful executive, it has been suggested, is a full in-basket in the morning and a full out-basket and waste basket at the end of the workday.

(6) **Vocabulary study.** Research on the vocabularies of executives has shown that they tend to be significantly larger than those of the average adult. Some successful business people with only high school educations surpass college seniors on vocabulary measures. This, then, is not so likely to be the underlying basis of inefficient reading habits for executives. However, if you find that you are frequently puzzled by words that occur in your everyday reading, you might embark on an

informal program of study.

The first step is to stop avoiding words you don't know. We have a way of ignoring unknown words, treating them literally as if they did not exist. You may have had the experience of suddenly acquiring a new word and then finding that this word crops up again and again almost as though its birth in your language was concurrent with your acquesition of it. You are on your way to acquiring a larger vocabulary when you begin to take note of these "new' words. Jot the word down as it occurs along with the phrase in which you found it for later consultation with the dictionary; or, if convenient, look it up on the spot.

One way to build your new word list is by entering single words on 3x5 cards with the word on one side and synonyms, definitions and illustrative uses on the other. From time to time you can test yourself on the words, discarding a word-card when you feel you have made the word your own. Attempt to use new words in speaking and writing. A word used spontaneously in this fashion three or four times is probably yours for life.

Here are a few rather difficult words that appear fairly frequently. Do you know their meanings? Could you use them easily and correctly?

primordial	simulate
burgeon	pristine
collateral	scrupulous
quiescence	obliterate
factitious	somnolent
anachronism	travesty
malingerer	delineate
predatory	colloquial

These sixteen words are, of course, a very small sampling, but if you know all but one or two of them, most likely your over-all effective vocabulary is good.

Chapter 4
The Sharpening of Your Memory and How It Helps You

Unlike your biceps, your memory is not a muscle which can be strengthened by exercise. When we admire the phenomenal ability of people to memorize dates, faces, names, facts and figures, we are dealing with a kind of learning ability which is a combination of several specific variables. Improvement in memorization comes mainly through knowing techniques of learning; and there may be different techniques for memorizing poetry and figures than for connecting names and faces correctly.

In this chapter we'll take a look at the learning process generally; then we'll turn to the specific human relations skills of mastering names and connecting them with the right faces.

Four Steps

In learning lessons in class, which we demonstrate by reciting or writing something upon demand, we are behaving in a certain way. Our writing muscles or our vocal chords move in specific correct ways which they couldn't have done without learning. This behavior change results from four progressive steps: (1) acquisition, (2) retention, (3) recognition, and (4) recollection.

Before we can remember anything we must have received the information, the image, or the data in the past. This is the **acquisition** stage. If the knowledge has not "gone in one ear and out the other," it has been **retained.** At some subsequent time–either a day, a week, or a month later–we **recognize** something which we have seen before, indicating that it has been retained. This means that it is familiar. "I know that hat; I saw it in church three years ago," you may say upon recognizing an object within a certain context. If, in helping your daughter learn a history lesson, you ask: "Who discovered America?" she may reply, "I know but I can't tell you." What she is saying is that she can't **recall** (call up again) the name of Christopher Columbus, which, of course, means that she doesn't know it. (If you can't **say** it, you don't **know** it.)

Let's look at each of these steps to learning in turn.

Acquiring New Knowledge

In intake, the rate of learning things, such as people's names or verses of poetry, follows a curve. Let's take the rate at which a person who is working at remembering names and faces in context can learn. You'll discover that your rate of learning and making such recognitions follows a curve and perhaps two.

Here's a typical learning curve found for one member of a course who plotted his progress over a period of time. When he starts, he find an immediate improvement in the number of faces he can connect with the right names in a strange group of 25 people one week after the first meeting in which he is introduced. The effectiveness goes up to a higher level with the second group, as he studies the technique and practices it. Finally there is a leveling off, or, as the statisticians call it, a negative acceleration. This means he keeps learning but not at as fast

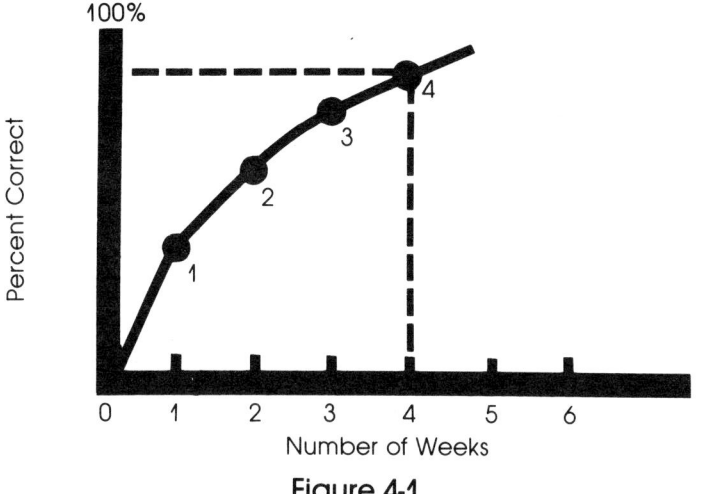

Figure 4-1

a rate as before. A sample learning curve for remembering faces is shown in Figure 4-1.

If you'd like to conduct an experiment, start rating your own ability to use memory pegs as learning tools. Take some groups you enter for the first time (perhaps adult education classes or church groups.) On your first meeting, try to master as many names and faces as possible, connecting the two through memory pegs. Attempt to recall them a week later. Use the chart in Figure 4-2 or another like it constructed on graph paper in your notebook to record the percentage of correctly matched names and faces by group after one week.

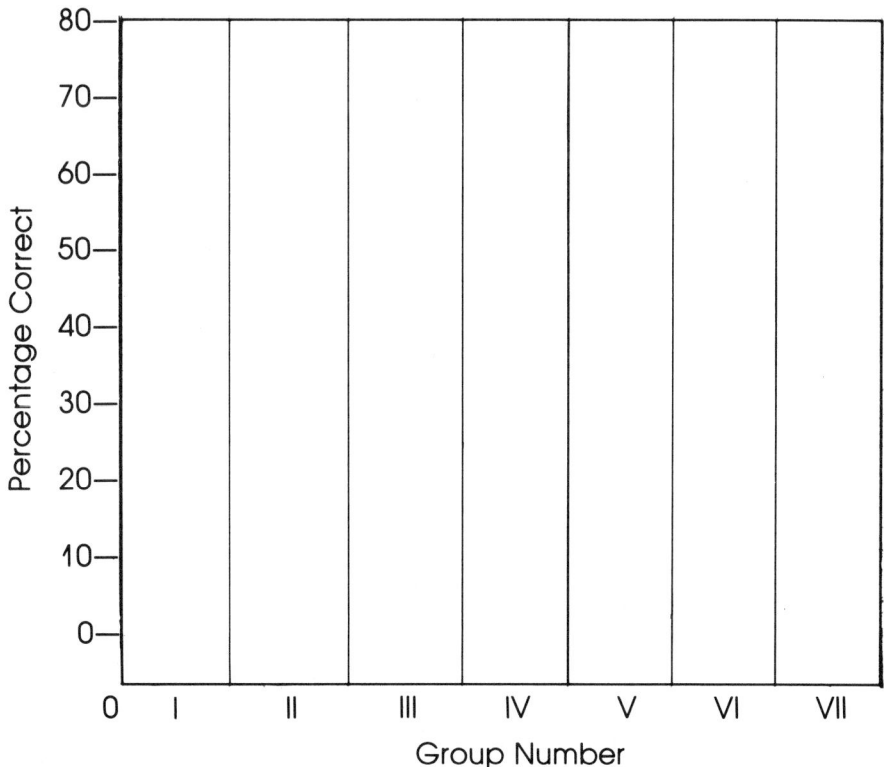

Figure 4-2

Just mix with your first group in the same way you have mixed with new groups in the past. One week later try to recall the names of as many people as possible and mark a dot on the chart above Group I. In the next new group you join (don't wait for one to show up, go find one), apply your memory word pegs, then try to recall as many names as possible for the same group a week later. Plot that one above Group II on the chart. Now draw a line between the two dots. Do this for four or more new groups. Each time apply your memory pegs skill and watch your learning curve emerge, sloping upward and to the right.

This is an important first step in improving your learning. **Watching your own learning curve as you learn has a positive motivational effect upon continued learning.**

You will see that there are some natural laws at work here which are in your favor. For example, you will notice that the longer you are in contact with each individual, the more apt you are to fix the memory word peg and to increase the likelihood of recalling the name when you see the face again. This will vary with people, of course, but you can acquire some skill if you plot your progress carefully.

After some first rapid gains, as you get onto the higher levels, the curve may begin to fluctuate and you may have little relapses in your progress. A learning plateau appears for some people and they level off for awhile, but, if they press on with their practice, they'll see their learning curve rise again. There is no real necessity for you to become a parlor trickster, but you should be able to select some key people in a group and remember all of them pretty well. Perhaps the big boss, a key customer, or a potentially useful one can be selectively chosen for fixation in your mind.

There are some rules which make for efficiency in acquiring things you hope to remember. They are well known, having been first discovered by the German psychologist Ebbinghaus back in 1885. They have subsequently been verified by many experiments and are as good today as ever. Although Ebbinghaus wasn't connecting names and faces, the basic memorization rules stand for that purpose.

Rule 1: Distributed learning is more effective than massed learning. You'll probably learn more by dividing the material to be learned into three bites over three days than by trying to learn it all on the last day. Ebbinghaus found that in learning syllables he remembered more from thirty-eight repetitions over three days than from sixty-eight repetitions the last day alone.

Rule 2: Meaningful things are easier to learn than meaningless things. If you are stowing away junk, you will be only one-eighth as efficient as when you are learning something useful. That means that your word pegs in memorizing names and faces will be much more effective for people important for you to remember than in fixing the faces of some fellow riders on a bus whom you'll never see again and wouldn't have any use for if you did know them. The old saying "I never forget a face, but in your case I'll make an exception" can reflect a desire to forget for some reason.

Rule 3: Rhythm and rhyming improve memorization. In written and in verbal fixation of a name with a face you'll find that it's easier to remember "Thomas Brewer is a Kalamazoo-er" than to recall that "Mr. Tom Brewer resides in the city of Kalamazoo, Michigan." I remember from my younger days in the army hearing a GI describe his date as "Cassie Massey with the classy chassis." Although more than thirty years have gone by, I recall the young lady well, although time may have altered her last name as well as her more memorable features.

Rule 4: Reciting improves effectiveness. If you want to fix the name, repeat it–if not to the person's face, at least to another person. This active participation is using the process aids the rate of learning.

In addition to these four memory rules, here are five guides to concentration which will serve you well in acquiring knowledge:

(1) Looking at a person is not enough. **Intend to learn** the person's name and face.

(2) **Muscular tension increases learning.** Strangely enough, there is scientific evidence that a mild increase in muscular toxicity sharpens learning. Relaxed, torpid, passive attention lowers learning. Tensing muscles, pressing your fingertips together if seated, and tightening other muscles (pressing your arms to your side, for example) increase the likelihood of learning a name and face.

(3) **Physical rewards and punishments affect learning.** Crushing a person's hand in a grip is more apt to cause a person to forget you than if you grip the person firmly without causing pain. Greeting people warmly rather than coolly also helps you to be remembered.

(4) **Praise and reproof affect learning.** You will be less apt to learn the person's name and recall it if you are snubbed or scolded than if the person is warm and complimentary toward you.

(5) **Emotional conditions affect learning.** The human body is made up of ten systems, including the skeletal, muscular, reproductive and integumentary (skin) systems. Two important systems that affect learning are the central nervous system and the glandular system (which is really a kind of chemical system for the body). These two systems come into play whenever we become emotionally stimulated. They usually operate in such a way that their aroused state bars learning. In some cases it is the subject matter being learned that kindles emotions. Perhaps it quickens our inhibitions, or perhaps it makes us mad. In either case, our learning effectiveness may fall off unless we realize that this can happen and we control the emotional impact.

Retaining What You've Learned

The heart of the memory problem for most of us doesn't seem at first to be the learning of the subject matter now, but the storing away for future reference. Here are a few results of some research studies in this field which can help you improve your score in this regard.

- **You can't develop a generally better "memory".** The ability to remember names and faces may not carry over to remembering dates and numbers or verses of poetry through generally strengthening your "memory muscles," since there are no such muscles. You might do better to concentrate on the basic principles of learning and memorizing and find the common components of each kind of memorization. Or, you might do still better to figure out that kind of memorization that suits you best and that best meets your personal needs for business, pleasure or self-improvement.

If you have no occasion to meet people and no need to remember their names and faces, there's small need for developing this specific kind of skill. (Most people who deal with others do need such skill, I might hasten to add.) In any event, your ability to memorize names and faces shouldn't be construed to be a generalized ability to remember everything. If you want to learn and remember long quotations from a poet you like you must treat this as a separate problem. Back in 1901 two experimental psychologists, Thorndike and Woodworth, found that a change in one human function doesn't result in a change in any other function except where the two functions have identical components.

- **Past learning may require unlearning.** An old habit which you've learned well through constant practice may take some unlodging before the new one can supplant it. If you have made it a practice never to look at people when you talk to them, you may have to break this habit before you start learning to connect names and faces, using memory word pegs. Back at the start of this century Hugo Munsterberg, the harvard psychologist, noted this interference of one habit with acquiring another and keeping it.

- **Retention is highest when you use the newly learned behavior.** Many people who received grades of straight A in mathematics when in college couldn't do a simple calculus problem today (if there is such a thing as s simple calculus problem, anyway). You hang onto learning more when you use it than when you don't use it.

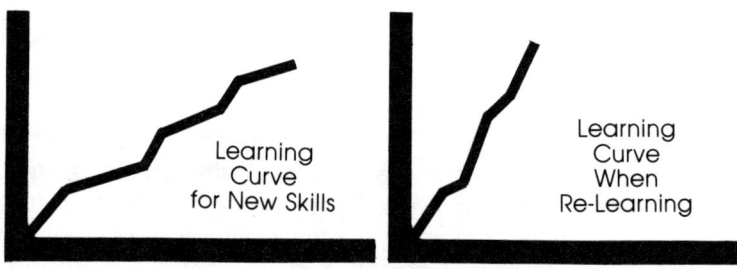

Figure 4-3

- **Relearning a forgotten skill is faster than original learning.** As you engage in a process of learning how to do something, you follow a learning curve which climbs upward in quite an orderly fashion. After many days, months, or even years, when you have apparently forgotten, learning once more will produce a much steeper curve. In other words, relearning and coming up to peak levels of memory will "come back quickly." The two curves in Figure 4-3 illustrate how your learning curve would look for fresh material and for familiar or previously learned material.

This is very important when memorizing peoples' names and faces. You may have fixed a group of names in your mind at one time but have been away from them for a short period of time or for several years. You'll find it much easier to master the old group than a new and different group.

- **Being forgetful doesn't mean that memories are "fading away."** The idea that a person's mind is a clean slate on which memories are written and can fade out just isn't valid. Experiments show that retention is better if the learning is followed immediately by a rest period rather than by some kind of active period in which other new events are seen and heard. For example, if you attend class one evening, proceed from there to a local bar where you see a stimulating show, then engage in a debate, and after that meet fifty people, you won't do as well in remembering what you heard in class as if you went home and hit the hay.

- **An uncompleted task will be remembered better than a completed one.** Psychologist Kurt Lewin conducted some experiments which showed that people who were interrupted halfway through a task remembered what had gone on before better than those who had completed tha task and wrapped it up. The tension which is created keeps the completed portion in your consciousness. If you are determined to learn the names, occupations and faces of twenty people in a room, but your spouse insists that you leave immediately ("you can complete your memory tricks tomorrow night, dear"), on the following night when you rejoin the group you'll remember those you met the previous day better than if you'd completed the job in one night.

Recalling and Reproducing Knowledge

The payoff from memorizing comes when we can recall and reproduce the material or facts or names we have learned. This leads us to several key points which can help you do a better job of reproducing what you learned previously.

- **Reproducing learned materials or facts is a reaction.** Certain kinds of outside stimuli trigger the memory. One word reminds us of another. For example, a word spoken by a friend "reminds me of the time when. . ." The stimulus might be physical. The string on your finger is an example of such a stimulus. A familiar odor may remind you of your childhood. A particular song may trigger memories of an early romance, and you can now describe something you had apparently forgotten for years. An old reaction, such as recalling a person's name, can be reawakened by the sound of the person's voice, or by some gesture or physical characteristic. This is the root of the word peg.

- **We reproduce things we've learned within a particular context.** The husband who never forgot his wife's birthday because it was the day Twenty Grand won the Wood Memorial does so because he is an avid horse race fan, not because he is an ardent lover. We tend to recall and reproduce an entire pattern; and fixing the entire pattern in learning increases the likelihood of recalling and reproducing a single event, face or name.

- **We learn things well when they solve a problem.** The organism which is in a state of disequilibrium (off balance) will recall things which "set things right." Your personal interest is enlisted when things don't seem to be on an even keel; and you'll tend to remember better those things which straighten you out and make you feel more comfortable. Your personal interest and need will guide your ability to reproduce past learning.

There are four laws of learning that are useful when it comes to the stage of recall and reproduction of memories. These laws can aid you in making your memory work better. They are: (1) the law of recency, (2) the law of frequency, (3) the law of primacy, and (4) the law of intensity.

The law of recency says that you'll remember something that happened close to the present. Students cram for tests, and singers protest that they haven't sung a particular song in years. This law may even lead you in the wrong direction. You will mis-label Mr. Shafter as Mr. Schaffer if you have met a Mr. Schaffer since you previously met Mr. Shafter.

The law of frequency says that if you repeat something you are more likely to remember it and be able to reproduce it. When you first meet a person it is a good idea to use the person's name several times. "Are you related to the Schaeffer's in Yonkers?" gives you a legitimate reason to discuss the name while you are watching the person's face, posture, mannerisms and the like.

The law of primacy says that first impressions are often lasting. You remember for many years the sergeant who swore you into the army or your first day on the job.

The law of intensity says that matters which are emphasized, dramatized or otherwise pounded home will be recalled and restated more easily at some future time. The teacher who whacks the desk or the preacher who shouts key points in a sermon attempts to use this law.

In summary, your memory isn't like your biceps, but you can master the procedures for strengthening it. As a beginner you might try recalling and reproducing the techniques outlined in this chapter. Use these techniques to learn the major points in the chapter; then try them in other situations and test them in practice.

Chapter 5
Constructing a Self-Image

We are constantly being bombarded with sensations. Sounds, smells, noises, words, pictures, sights and tactile feelings press upon us all day long. These things all fall under the heading of "experience." It has been suggested in the last chapter that we are affected in many ways by these stimuli or experiences. The bird whose sensory apparatus informs him that the days are getting shorter prepares to fly south for the winter. The driver who sees the amber light prepares to stop her car for the red light to follow.

At the same time, we know that people are not simple windup toys ("push my action button and watch me run"). Inside of us there takes place a process by which we choose, organize and interpret sensory stimuli. These make up a coherent picture of the whole world. This image of the world includes everything we know. It has an important function. It determines our reaction to sensory bullets that hit us from outside ourselves.

The flight crew in the cockpit of a plane has an image that helps them organize incoming messages which they receive through their eyes (other planes on the horizon), their ears (landing instructions from the tower), and their hands (on the controls). The thing that makes these people different from some untrained person who might find himself or herself at the controls is that they have an image which includes all of their past training and experience and its organization.

Where Your Self-Image Comes From

In addition to your image of the world around you, you have an image of yourself. this isn't in isolation from the world but is part of it. Your image includes both the world and your situation as well as yourself. You receive information from the world as messages. When such a message hits, as Kenneth Boulding points out, it can have three possible effects upon your image:

1. The message may whiz right on through and leave your image unaffected. Most mesages do this. We hardly hear the regular noise around us, since we do many things from habit and accomodate to screening out some messages automatically.

2. It might change your image in some regular, well-defined way. A reverie is interrupted by the honking of a car horn, indicating that your car pool is sitting impatiently in front of your house awaiting your presence. You go from a world of pleasant-perhaps sleepy-reverie to a world of urgency and haste. This happens every morning.

3. Or it may have such an impact that it rearranges the whole image. A religious conversion, a revealing book, or a germinal Idea by a teacher or preacher sometimes has this kind of an effect upon our image. At such times we say that the image has been reorganized, which is a happy way of saying that our self-image can be changed, and that such changes in image will change behavior. These changes often seem to be startling leaps forward (or backward); but, in fact, they are relatively small in terms of the total amount of data which is encompassed in the existing image.

An idea, or a new way of seeing things, can affect us in such a way as to change our image of ourselves. Abraham Maslow, the psychologist, helped us see other people in a new light with his "hierarchy of needs." We start looking at a friend and try to guess which need he or she is trying to alleviate by a particular action that the person has taken. (Maslow's hierarchy of needs idea will be described in detail in Chapter 7.)

Thus the sources of our images are outside ourselves, and these images are a form of energy which impinges upon us. Our image is far less often affected by isolating ourselves from outside sensations. A vacation trip where we see new things, new faces, hear new tongues, and experience new sensations is more apt to alter our image than is retiring to our study and staring at the wall. In fact, such a "think tank" isolation often does nothing more than cause the elements in our image to flip-flop around like a TV picture tube with the horizontal control button out of kilter. I should hasten to add, however, that reading a book in isolation isn't in the same category. Locked in a cell you may commune with Plato or Thomas Aquinas and experience the joyous input of new ideas and new arrangements of them.

Since we have higher and lower tolerances for new sensations, not every experience affects us to the same extent. We know from psychological experiments that human receptivity to sensations changes as it is required to keep its balance. Constant receipt of sensation dulls our sensitivity to it. People are observed plunging into the ocean off Cape Cod which seems unbearably frigid to the visitor from Florida who is paralyzed by merely inserting a big toe into the water. The capacity of the soldier to continue in combat, or the surgeon to work without nausea at the sight of blood and viscera, is a happy product of this decreasing sensitivity. The inexperienced person is often more sensitive than an experienced, "toughened" person.

What Your Image Does For You

Sensations alone, or raw facts alone, can't produce a coherent picture of the world including your place in it. Some experiences will come to you with no discernible effect on either your image or your behavior–they are screened out or allowed to whiz right on through, as already noted. This screening out process is an important part of your image, and, as we've seen, your image affects your behavior. Your behavior will have a decided effect upon your sucess.

Three factors involved in screening will determine what you include in your image, or reject from it (allow to fly on by):

1. The kind of message itself is important. Repetitious, boring, uninteresting material, or material which seems to be unpleasant or threatening in a minor sort of way, is apt to be screened out and never affects your image when it is completely rejected.

2. Prior learning will set up some screens and filters for learning. The person who has learned that all members of the opposite sex are deceitful and cruel will not be enticed by a smile.

3. Your emotional state and your motives will facilitate the screening out of certain messages. When you have a goal of making a million

dollars and there is some opportunity in sight, the chance for some minor pleasure seems worthless and you screen it out. The ardent suitor is apt to screen out small evidences of disapproval from his or her future in-laws and, perhaps, even from the person being pursued.

Messages then have a variable impact upon the receiver, determining whether or not they will chage a person's behavior. The needs of the individual will be as important in operating one' selectivity apparatus for new ideas, new sensations and new stimuli as the quality of the ideas or sensations themselves. The person who is enrolled in an evening course by his or her boss under protest may stoutly maintain to the instructor that"You can't teach me anything." This is indeed true. In enlarging your image you can do it only if you need to enlarge it and know that you have this need.

You might say we set up "perceptual defenses," illustrated by the old saw, "None is so blind as he who will not see." In short, you won't learn it unless you have determined to make such learning your goal.

The First Step in Constructing An Image

The primary step in creating a better image (which is the basis of much of your behavior) is to set a goal for yourself in terms of what you would like to be and what you would like to know. You can't be a doctor without studying medicine, nor a lawyer without studying law. This means you must first determine what you want, then seek out the messages which will "flesh out" the image.

Dr. William Glasser, a California psychiatrist, reports on a patient who was failing in college and felt that life was empty. By working on his school problems and solving them by setting some goals the doctor was able to help the young man see himself as someone different. He even found that his goal of becoming a medical doctor was not impossible, once he had determined his goal. With the goal in mind, his grades improved, even in scientific subjects for which he had previously felt he lacked aptitude.

The first step in image building then is to sketch an accurate perception of yourself and some of your present problems.

The Fabric of Your Image

The facts about yourself don't comprise your image. The latter includes needs that you feel and values that you hold important. This is an excellent time to define for yourself your own needs according to the hierarchy outline of physical needs, ego needs, social needs, and self-actualizing or self-expressive needs. You might try sketching out some of your own needs at this time in Figure 5-2. Think of things you'd like to have that you don't–things you'd like to obtain, contribute or take part in.

Using this outline permits you to spell out some of your own values and work out tangible plans for meeting your needs.

"But suppose I don't make them, won't I be disappointed?" is a common question. True, you'll be disappointed; but you'll also achieve some successes and these will be rewarding enough to take care of the disappointments over failure. It also helps if you realize that disappointment is a normal condition for everyone who sets high standards.

As philosopher Bertrand Russell has put it, "You find happiness by turning your passions outward, not looking inward." Don't sit around staring at your navel and worrying about your weaknesses. Start by clarifying your needs, convert them into goals and get to work moving toward those goals. Even if you never arrive, you'll find yourself so busy pursuing the goals you'll forget yourself, and, as you look back on those busy days, you'll realize they were your happiest.

Your image is the goals you are pursuing; and the kind of person you are is shaped by your unfulfilled projects.

Category	Some specific goals in each category which would represent goal achievement
1. Physical needs: List such things as salary level, house, car vacations, marriage, a library, a den, membership in a club and the like. **Your plan for achieving these needs:** a. List the objective. b. What are the steps needed to get there? c. What is the timing for each step? d. What obstacles will you face on the way? e. What plan do you have for getting around, over or through the obstacle? f. If it is insurmountable, what alternative goal could you pick to achieve the same need fulfillment? g. How will you know (by what indicators) that you've achieved this objective?	1.
2. Ego Needs Publicity, reputation, name in magazines, radio interviews, people saying favorable things about you, nobody saying bad things, etc. **Your plan for achieving these needs:** a. List the objective. b. What are the steps needed to get there? c. What is the timing for each step? d. What obstacles will you face on the way? e. What plan do you have for getting around, over or through the obstacle?	2. Your specific targets

Category	Some specific goals in each category which would represent goal achievement
f. If it is insurmountable, what alternative goal could you pick to achieve the same need fulfillment? g. How will you know (by what indicators) that you've achieved this objective? 3. Social needs: People you'd like to meet socially, clubs you'd like to join, invitations you'd like to get, memberships, number of parties and dinners attended, etc. **Your plan for achieving these needs:** a. List the objective. b. What are the steps needed to get there? c. What is the timing for each step? d. What obstacles will you face on the way? e. What plan do you have for getting around, over or through the obstacle? f. If it is insurmountable, what alternative goal could you pick to achieve the same need fulfillment? g. How will you know (by what indicators) that you've achieved this objective? 4. Self-actualizing Needs Talents you'd like to develop, painting, writing, building, creations you'd like to achieve, etc. **Your plan for achieving these needs:** a. List the objective. b. What are the steps needed to get there? c. What is the timing for each step? d. What obstacles will you face on the way? e. What plan do you have for getting around, over or through the obstacle? f. If it is insurmountable, what alternative goal could you pick to achieve the same need fulfillment? g. How will you know (by what indicators) that you've achieved this objective?	1. Your specific targets 2. Your specific needs

Figure 5-2

PART III
MOVING THINGS, PEOPLE AND SITUATIONS

Being ready for action and having a sound plan are merely prologues to the action which follows. The test comes when you confront the real world with its immovable objects, its people who want the same desirable benefits, and its complex situations which must be managed.

Chapter 6
Understanding the Activity Trap and How to Avoid It

As the world grows more complicated and certainly more densely populated it becomes more difficult to find reality. In an earlier day in small-town America reality was something easy to see. It consisted of the red dirt of Georgia, black loam of Wisconsin, rocky hills of New England, clapboard houses, green grass, main streets and buckboard wagons.

Today we find reality is increasingly more complicated. Education has enlarged our skills. Knowledge has expanded, and is more ambiguous. Our interpersonal relationships are more complex.

We now have a great need to simplify this reality by finding a new way to look at things. Nowhere is this more true than in business where complex, multinational conglomerates employ persons in thousands of occupations. The simplifying explanatory device we have focused on is that of the "systems approach."

Using the Systems Approach

Now it may seem arrogant or even presumptuous in view of the complexity that's been growing up around us to say that we have a system that will explain everything. But this is exactly what the systems approach claims as its purpose. If it were only partially successful it would be quite valuable.

The particular system to be considered here is described as cybernetic system. We need to look at what it is, how it works, and how it can help you develop your personal effectiveness by keeping your eyes on things that are really important.

The three elements of the system are: (1) input, (2) activity and (3) output.

When we put any sort of business, government agency or social organization together we start out with certain kinds of resources which we put in. These, quite understandably then, are called **inputs** by the systems experts.

What are the inputs? An essential one is capital. It is converted into factories and offices, materials, machinery, supplies, and working capital (cash, receivables and inventories). Inputs are required to get the organization going.

Having our inputs, we next do something with them. We engage in buying and selling, engineering, manufacturing, writing reports, and so on. As the organization grows in size, these **activities** become more complex so we end up with various specialists in traffic, legal, purchasing, personnel administration, public relations, and the like.

As a result of the activities upon the inputs, those inputs are converted into something more valuable. This **output** should be greater than what was consumed in the process of making it.

This comprises the economics of the organization. Activity upon the resources or inputs produces **value added** which can be plowed back into the operation of the business or nonprofit organization, or, in the case of a business, it can be distributed to stockholders as

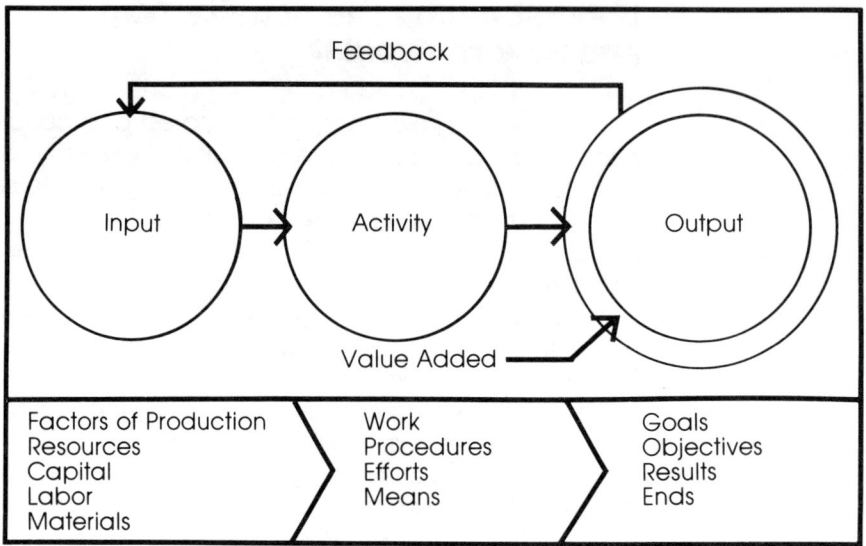

Figure 6-1

dividends.

These three simple elements, illustrated in Figure 6-1, comprise the language to be used to explain the complex thing we call business. Economists have been talking for more then two hundred years about the factors of production–land, labor and capital. But only in recent years when systems analysis has been applied to space age technology have we found the successful application of the systems approach to the management of corporations. Though it is nothing new, it is easy to see how the model fits all sorts of organizations, not just business.

The Activity Trap

Although this simple system shows how an organization or a person could work, it leads one to the discovery that there apparently are some built-in traps in ongoing human systems. These are input traps, activity traps and output traps. Of the three, perhaps the activity trap is the most pervasive reason for why organizations and people fail.

People start out for what were once important objectives, but, in an amazingly short period of time, they become so enmeshed in the activity of their jobs the activity becomes a false goal. The outputs aimed for–such as adding value to things, creating a profit, delivering service to veterans, delivering the mail, or providing health care for people–are lost when the original reason for which inputs were committed are forgotten.

> **In the activity trap, activity becomes an end in itself and people lose sight of their purpose for performing the activity.**

We will find, for example, that school systems consume inputs, engage in activities, and presumably produce as their "output" educated children who possess certain skills and values. But somehow this is not happening, and that's why many people are unhappy about their school systems. The school system consumes resources and its teachers and administrators engage in lots of activity, but the "output" in terms of educated children seems to fall short of expectations.

Governments, too, are apparently under this same demonic spell of the activity trap. The inputs which they keep demanding from taxpayers go up and up, but the quality and amount of service given seems to be deteriorating in many cases. The costs of federal, state and local government has tripled over a decade and no one seems any happier for it. The ability of governments to consume limitless resources seems to be linked to being caught up in a massive activity trap producing outputs that are totally unrelated to what the public wants.

Hospitals and health care service agencies likewise find themselves under a cloud. Resources are put in, activity is engaged in, but the average length of life in the United States has declined with respect to the averages in other countries. What is wrong here that such an important output indicator should show a decline while inputs are rising so astronomically?

Social clubs seem to be afflicted with the same kinds of trouble. Dues of members keep going up, and the amount of activity demanded of members is on the rise: "Let's all get out and support old Joe in this activity because he's worked hard planning it." Never mind whether the activity is one that the members want or need.

Even the family seems to find itself caught in this systems dilemma of the activity trap. The mechanics or activity of living have replaced the purposes of living.

Identifying Successful Personal Behavior

Perhaps now we can identify what the successful people do that the unsuccessful ones don't do. Certainly it is apparent that there must be something different about the behavior of successful people that causes them to produce the kinds of output that are wanted which others aren't able to achieve.

The only apparent difference that we can see on the surface between successful and unsuccessful people is that the successful are successful and the unsuccessful are unsuccessful. This is a tautology. That is, something equals itself. You might not think that this is a very substantial basis for teaching you how to be successful, but if we press on you can see that the explanation is reasonably simple. At least the problem is clear.

Unsuccessful people are caught up in the activity trap. They've become so enmeshed in activity they've lost sight of why they are doing what they are doing and the activity has become an end in itself. At first this is a momentary lapse, then it's a bad habit, next it becomes a procedure, and finally it's a religion.

Unlike the unsuccessful person, a successful person never loses sight of his or her goals. This is what makes them successful and it's the one characteristic that

distinguishes them from the unsuccessful.

It's like a design in the wall paper you couldn't see before it was pointed out. The activity trap increases our understanding of what has gone wrong, and clarifies what must be done to make things go right.

If what you are doing is right, it means that you do not have to change your behavior. Still, you should do this consciously and should teach it to others so they don't fall into the activity trap.

Falling into the activity trap is not a function of intelligence or personality. It is a natural tendency to start out for once visible, once important, once exciting objectives. But, as practical persons, we naturally get going on doing something about them, and often get lost in the activity of what we are doing.

The most successful people have mastered the ability to keep their eyes on objectives and goals at the same time as they carry on complex activities. How does one avoid the activity trap? By seeing the answers to two questions at once: (1) What are the purposes of this organization? (2) What do I have to do to achieve them?

What are the practical effects of the activity trap in business. . . and in your life? It produces a quality control manager who behaves as if the entire business were designed so it could be shut down. It creates a production manager who sees the purpose of the organization as being that maximum volume can be shoved out the back door regardless of the quality or usefulness of the product. It produces accountants who behave as if the organization exists so they can keep books on it. It yields sales managers who say there is no problem that a little more volume won't solve, even while the firm is losing money on a substantial portion of what is being sold.

The activity trap shifts emphasis from the goal to the activity. It's not that activity is unneccessary. But it can only be valuable or useless according to its contribution to objectives. Where activity becomes a false goal we find organizations that consume resources and produce activity instead of outputs.

This produces a certain style of living in which "be active" is more important than "be productive." It says "do things my way" rather than "produce my results."

Some supervisors will say, "Yes, but don't you have to control the activity in order to control the output?" Not necessarily. Andrew Carnegie, one of the great organizers at the turn of the century, said when he got to ten steel mills he discovered he couldn't see everything that was going on in all of them, and that it was damaging to try. This is an amazing insight which many people could learn to their advantage today. Our ways of working are too frequently a means of generating activity rather than directing outputs. Time cards, close supervision and autocratic bosses are all evidences of the grip of the activity trap.

"But," you say, "don't people have to be active?" Yes, but there are high yield activities and low yield activities. High yield activities are those that make the greatest contribution to objectives.

"Yes," you say, "but don't I have to produce more activity to be effective?" No. What do you do if people do things the wrong way and get better results?

The activity-centered person is not only concerned with the volume of activity, but also sets up a system for reinforcing activity and creates a set of manners for engaging in that activity. These manners become obsessions. A resultant view is expressed in the statement that "My job is more important than the reason it was started." Of course no one would ever say this, but they behave as if they believe it.

Old activities take on an air of respectability which militates against innovation. Traditions and procedures become stabilizers that insure old activities prevail. Personnel officers write job descriptions that describe activities instead of outputs. Then, from fear of a pay cut or loss of a job, people won't change their activities. People who have creative interests are stopped cold in their tracks by the activity-centered lives they lead.

Despite the stranglehold that the activity trap has in all areas of human endeavor, it doesn't provide satisfaction or meet the needs of most people.

Ingredients Of Effectiveness

Avoiding the activity trap is called effectiveness. Perhaps the only pure act of leadership lies in goal setting and getting others to accept the goals and work toward them. If you have the ability to find goals and to get others committed to them, you are leading and let all of the other things follow.

When President John F. Kennedy set a goal of putting a man on the moon by 1970 he demonstrated a kind of results-centered leadership that characterized the sixties. The goal commanded the resources and activities of engineers, managers, taxpayers and legislators without major complaint because it struck the imagination of millions of people. This is the action of leadership.

The leader must define new objectives as they emerge, must explain them to people under him or her, must persuade them of a need for change in an orderly fashion, and must lead them towards the goals. Leadership must always have these six basic ingredients:

(1) Some worthy goals, which people are heading for.

(2) The commitment of people towards obtaining these goals. (A commitment is a kind of promise you make to someone whose opinion is important to you.)

(3) The acceptance of responsibility for behaving in ways that contribute to the achievement of these goals.

(4) The support and assistance in the effort to obtain the goals includes skill development and goal-centered activities.

(5) People should be allowed to have a sense of mastery and a satisfactory self-image when they achieve their goals.

(6) People need some time to engage in simple, purposeless activity for its own sake.

People Shrinkers

As the dominant institution in our society, corporations are a pretty important influence for governing our activities. In effect, the corporation produces the activity-centered society in which we live. Governments, homes, churches and voluntary associations all follow the lead of the corporations when it comes to shrinking the human potential of people.

When activity takes the place of objectives, resources are wasted and people shrink. We end up being so busy we don't have time to figure out the meaning of what we are doing. Millions of people go to work day after day and disappear promptly at starting time into their job descriptions and aren't seen again until quitting time.

How do people shrink in the activity trap? One way to see this is to try a little test of communication on objectives with your boss, with one of the people who work for you, or with your spouse.

First, working independently, each person should make up a separate list of your major areas of responsibility.

Second, also working independently, each of you should list what it is that you plan to actually produce within the next twelve months in each area of responsibility.

Third, compare the two lists.

Should they be in agreement? Clearly. Are they in agreement? Probably not. The average manager and subordinate left to their own devices are going to fail to agree on what is expected of the subordinate at a level of twenty-five to thirty per cent of the regular, ordinary and ongoing responsibilities. The level of disagreement is even higher in areas of problem solving and innovative responsibilities.

Is this disagreement bad? No, it is monstrous! Here's why: If you are the subordinate and fail to agree in advance of the period as to what is expected in terms of output at a level of thirty per cent, what is the maximum you could succeed in working for that boss on that job during that year? If you are in agreement on seventy per cent and fail to agree on thirty per cent, the maximum success you could achieve would be seventy per cent... even if you put out one hundred per cent of your best efforts, talents and abilities. In effect, you are enrolled in a course where your final grade has been discounted thirty points before you began!

People shrink when they don't know what is expected, when they cannot find out, and when they have a built-in failure rate even when they perform at one hundred per cent efficiency. People caught up in the activity trap ask: "Does anybody up there know what I want to do? Do they know what I can do? Do they even know what I am doing?

What can be done to break out of the activity trap? People should sit down with each other and talk about objectives to decide what will be produced during the coming period and how it will be evaluated. The agreement should then be confirmed by a memo. This process fits husbands and wives, parents and children, and club members and officers as well as it fits bosses and subordinates.

Chapter 7
Understanding Other People To Get Things and People Going Your Way

Modern behavioral science has produced many new insights into human behavior. In fact, research studies which explain and define human behavior are going on all the time. Research centers at major universities spend millions annually studying various facets of human behavior. They try to find out what causes consumers to buy (or to hoard), what makes voters act the way they do at the polls, and what makes engineers act like engineers.

Specific details of all of this research can be pretty technical. To read this you'd find yourself wrapped up in statistical calculation, tests of significance, two-tailed tests and the like. For our purposes, suffice it to say that you needn't be a scientist, psychologist or sociologist to tap this rich body of knowledge and to apply it to your action in day-to-day living to make yourself more effective.

In this chapter you'll find a model which will help you explain human behavior. This is pretty useful knowledge when the time comes to act–to move things along where other people must be moved along with you. You see, if you understand human behavior, you can do a better job of predicting what other people's behavior will be. If you can predict what it will be, this gives you a means of controlling the events ahead, for you'll be able to allow for the future. You might even be able to control that behavior by making allowances for it and perhaps by changing it. This is what the study of human relations is about.

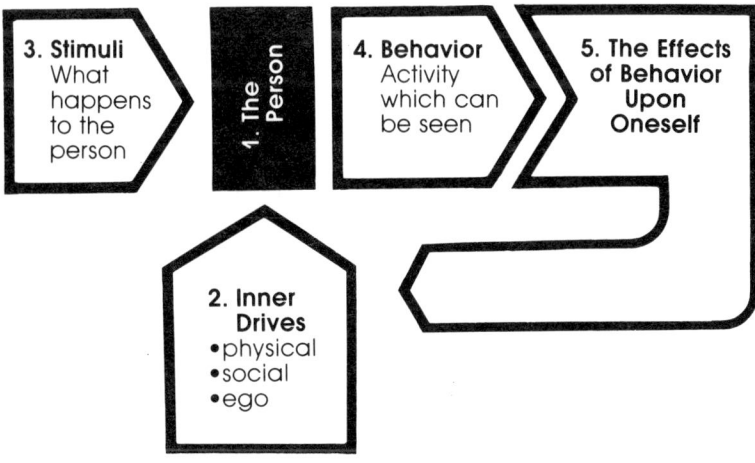

Figure 7-1

Our model for understanding human behavior (Figure 7-1) is one I've developed for this book; it isn't one the scientists invented. Clearly, the underlying theories are much more complex, but the basic ingredients in this model are all scientifically sound. Let's look at the components that make up this model: (1) At the crossroads is the person. (2) Inside the person are certain drives which compel him or her to behave in a certain way. (3) From outside there are cues and prods–we call them stimuli–which move the person in one direction or another. Sometimes the inner drives and stimuli occur simultaneously as when a person is hurrying across a street to meet a friend and is honked at by a car horn. (4) What follows these stimuli is what the person does as a result of the stimulus being applied–we call it "behavior." Behavior is tangible; you can see it, measure it, count it, take a picture of it, or record it in some way. The definition of behavior is "activity which can be seen or measured." (5) Once the person has behaved in a certain way, some result caused by the behavior occurs. A person touches a hot stove and immediately finds that his or her hand is burned, for example.

These five ingredients, all surrounding and affecting the person, comprise the subject of this chapter and the action model for understanding human behavior.

The Hierarchy Of Needs

Man is an animal and has all of the characteristics of a mammal, but is not limited to those conditions. Human beings have the skeletal, circulatory, muscular, integumentary, reproductive, nervous, glandular and digestive systems of other mammals. This isn't intended to be a medical text, but the physical make-up of people is closely related to the explanations of their behavior. It's apparent that changes in our physical plants affect everything else about us. A high fever, a serious injury, or four double martinis will transform any one of us into a different person for the duration of the change.

It's not a bad idea to look here first when you see significant changes in yourself or in your close friends. When you feel lazy, or when there is a change in your outlook, a check-up with your physician is probably a sensible first step. If you find that all's well here, the next step is to turn to the needs you have at a psychological level. These needs appear to fall into a hierarchy; that is, when one of them is satisfied, the next highest comes into play and becomes urgent.

• **Physical needs** take precedence over others. People who are very hungry or very thirsty probably will pay little heed to social or ego needs like social standing and pride. They will make any move that is necessary to satisfy that physical need for water or food. Once that need is satisfied, however, the whole person is not necessarily satisfied. Another kind of need rises into a more prominent position. This can be illustrated in a pair of diagrams.

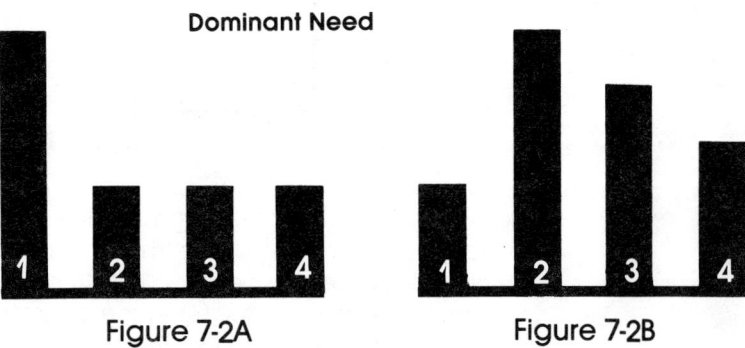

Figure 7-2A   Figure 7-2B

In Figure 7-2A the subject has an unfilled physical need that takes a dominant position in affecting the person's behavior. In Figure 7-2B we see what happens when that phsyical need has been satisified. Another need which was previously subordinated rises into the dominant position. The person now wishes to satisfy this need; and the effects of this unsatisfied need are just as great in shaping behavior as those of the previously unsatisfied physical need.

Once people have satisfied most of their physical needs, they will still remain desirous of finding social, egotistical or self-actualizing (self-expresseve) satisfactions.

We should note that an unsatisfied need is an internal cause of a person's outward behavior and that without needs a person would become a vegetable. A satisfied need is not a motivator, and people always have new needs. Most of our physical needs are met in our affluent society. This doesn't mean that we are without needs, however. Social, ego and self-expressive needs are constantly pressing us for more goals to be achieved.

- **Egotistical needs** are those which make people feel important to themselves. People feel that their sense of worth and liking for themselves call for certain kinds of behavior on the part of others. As a practical matter, this drive in people means that we avoid those actions which rob others of self-esteem. Rob a person of self-respect and in defense he or she must react in kind. For a boss to deride an employee in public, to downgrade his or her efforts, or to belittle the subordinate reduces the possibility of getting that person's best efforts. Subordinates will turn their attention to getting even with the boss and hating him or her, rather than trying to help the boss achieve his or her goals.

- **Social needs** grow out of what psychologists call the instinct for gregariousness. This means simply that people are social animals, like to be with other people, and need the companionship and friendship of others. The worst form of punishment for a normal person is to be isolated from human contact. If this isolation is forced on a person and extended, he is she is said to be "alienated," and personal effectiveness drops. The simple human value of being friendly and extending kindly words has the same effect as stroking a pet. We all like what psychologist Eric Berne calls "stroking behavior" in others, and we like to get it in return when we extend it to others. Saying "good morning" to everyone is a kind of necessary social cement that makes the condition of being born an individual more bearable. Letting people know you recognize them as members of the group, making them feel "in," is an important key to effective human relations. Simple stuff? Surely. Yet it's sufficiently important to all of us that without it we die a little.

- **Self-actualizing needs** are rather difficult to define and involve different things for different people. Every person has a kind of activity at which he or she feels adequate, or at which he or she can do better than most people. It may be running a lathe, tying a trout fly, chipping shots onto the green with an eight iron, fixing a gourmet dinner, developing new products, or writing useful analytical reports. This need to express ourselves through something we do is a basic need in normal people. Bosses who deny employees opportunity to express themselves on the job kill initiative, incentive, productivity and creativity.

Affecting People's Behavior By Meeting Their Needs

The important point about this hierarchy of needs is that such needs are common to normal people, and they afford us clues to predicting the behavior of others and to getting others to do things we'd like them to do. Why shouldn't they? You are helping them at a fundamental level. We shouldn't underestimate the power to affect people through meeting their needs. Often they will sacrifice many valuable hours, preferences, or even tangible possessions for the person who helps them retain their human capacities through meeting these needs.

Demagogues, manipulators, con men, and great lovers have often mastered this knowledge and used it to exploit people. The needs are neutral, and their use is under the control of the user. They naturally should be used for ethical purposes. Yet, knowing about them means one can avoid being manipulated, and, at the same time, can use them for good purposes.

Suppose you decide that your knowledge of human relations permits you to "con" people into going against their own long-term interests. Almost inevitably you will acquire such an unenviable reputation that you will be mistrusted.

Thus, this knowledge of human behavior and motives should be coupled with a general value system of using it to help others rather than to exploit them to their own disadvantage, or the entire system will merely serve to damage your own reputation. The fictional character of Sergeant Bilko on TV was recognized by all as exploitative; at the same time we could marvel at his ability to size up the raw humanity of his appeal and his skill in using an extensive knowledge of human behavior to trick others. We could see through his machinations and laugh at the innocence of others. This ability to see our motives as we apply our human relations skill to affecting the behavior of others is far more widespread than is supposed.

Chapter 8
The Importance of Clear Goals

Plenty of young people have energy and drive but never seem to get anywhere. They race back and forth frantically with this idea or that, fixing first upon one scheme and then upon another. Small wonder they end up frustrated at age forty, missing out on the big chances that seem to fall to lesser men and women. People who fix their eyes on a single target, or a brace of related targets, can plod along at their daily round, each day gaining over the "grasshopper" people.

The most important aspect of getting action isn't motion or activity; it is purpose, goals and targets.

Results Are More Important Than Activity

The modern approach to management in the largest corporations and in the federal government since the days of Robert MacNamara is what is called the "systems approach." Perhaps you won't be Secretary of Defense, but you can use a systems approach to getting things done in your own life, job, home or social affairs.

A system has three major ingredients: (1) Clear identification of your objectives, including the spelling out of some indicators of success or failure in achieving them. (2) Definition and control of your activities according to the way in which each contributes to your objective. (3) Rationing of your resources of time, energy and money into those activities that will make the best use of them. Let's look at each of these in turn.

Identification of Your Objectives

The first step in identifying an objective is to find out where you are at the present time and to choose some place better you would like to be at some specific time in the future. You've made a pretty good start if you have worked out the exercise in Chapter 5, but there's more if you are going to develop an action plan that works.

- You will find it useful to list the inescapable routine things with which you'll be faced first. If you must support a husband or wife, children, or an aging parent, you put that down first. Few civilized persons would emulate the painter Gauguin and run away from such responsibilities in order to pursue a career as a painter.

- In listing these regular responsibilities, show the eight to ten major areas of responsibility which will comprise your routine maintenance tasks for the coming year or two. List them in order of importance. Also list all those that will be in conflict with one another. These are your "trade-off" objectives. For example, you might have a burning desire to continue bowling with your league, but bowling conflicts with your desire to get a college education at night. Something has to give. You must trade off one objective against the other.

- Don't get too wedded to everything in your Category I objectives list (Figure 8-1) because you are now going to start mapping out your improvement objectives. In order to pay for them out of your resources of money, time, energy and talent you may have to lop off some of the lower priority items of the routine kind.

Category I: Regular, Routine or Maintenance Objectives

Key Results Areas	Indicators of success or failure for this objective		
Major Areas (Example: food and rent)	**Poor** fall behind $150/wk	**Satisfactory** make ends $200/wk	**Excellent** have some $250/wk
1.			
2.			
3.			
4.			
5.			
6.			
7.			
8.			
9.			
10.			
11.			

In this category list the inescapable things you must do while you are also making some breakthroughs in the personal improvement areas which follow. List the priorities and be ready to trade away the lower priorities later if need be.

Figure 8-1

Category II: Personal Development Plan.

a. List the new goal you'd like to achieve: Why do you want it?	
b. List some of the steps along the way.	
Stage	**Expected Date for Achievement**
1.	
2.	
3.	
4.	
5.	
6.	
7.	
8.	

You might find a separate **objectives notebook** would be sensible at this stage. You may have to construct two or three such personal improvement sheets. Note also that you'll be making adjustments in your Categroy I statement, if needed, in order to pay for this plan.

Figure 8-2

performing well, albeit unhappily. He couldn't attend evening school because his selling required much evening work, but he was able to take a correspondence course in business law and claims adjustment. Having made a distinguished record in this area, he applied for a position in the claims department. The change required him to take a reduction in pay, but now he is back at his former income level and has risen to claims manager in regional office. Most importantly, he is doing what he likes and will probably succeed at it.

There are some generalizations that can be made from this case. Person A stands before two propositions that have varying degrees of attractiveness. On the one hand, the person might continue in his or her present position. In so doing, the person can continue to be successful, can maintain his or her current level of income, and won't have to undergo the extra trouble of studying a new course and then entering a new field where a risk of failure exists. On the other hand, the person may choose a new career in which the work is more fascinating, where the hours and working conditions are good, and where the opportunities for growth and advancement look better.

Two different sets of "field forces" are pressing the individual. Presuming that they are equally strong the person may choose a course of action in which neither of the two alternatives are achieved. The salesman, for instance, may have been so bemused by his desire to become a claims manager that he would be unable to sell and would get himself fired. On the other hand, he could be so tied to selling by the fear of lost income that he couldn't make up his mind to jump into the claims field. In an illustration of the old saying that "the grass always appears to be greener on the other side of the fence," the fact that the person is already at one position may make the alternative position more attractive.

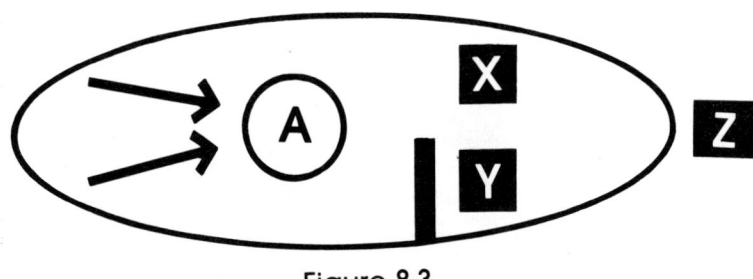

Figure 8-3

Beyond this simple choice situation there exists another important factor. The person exists within a "field." This means that people see certain limitations and boundaries around the situation, themselves, and their choices. This is illustrated in Figure 8-3 in which the field forces or "vectors" pressing upon Person A are shown as arrows, the barriers to choosing either X or Y are shown as a bar, and the outside limitations and boundaries are shown as an oval. Person A is bound by a set of general conditions such as age, family, home mortgage, car payments, and other factors that are accepted as given. Within that

Definition Your Personal Improvement Objectives

With your Category I objectives in hand you have defined your present condition or the condition to which you could adjust. It should be noted that these objectives aren't entirely personal since they may involve responsibilities which you have to others and from which you simply cannot walk away. To some extent you will have to involve others in these statements, since they may have to help you pay the price for bettering things for the future.

In outlining your Category II personal development objectives (Figure 8-2), there are several things to be kept in mind.

- Usually personal improvement goals are more than a single step long; they are multi-stage objectives. You may find, for example, that you need to go to college in order to get the job you'd really like. But, because of your maintenance objectives (family, mortgage, etc.), you will have to do this in evening college. This means that you must make up certain courses which you didn't take in high school and must pass the college admissions test. Thus, as you see, getting a particular new job may entail a chain of objectives.

- You start by defining the reason for wanting to improve; then work out the means of arriving at the desired outcome. For example, you might want to become a manager—to live a manager's life and earn a manager's pay. Your personal improvement plan, then, is based on the goal you set for yourself.

Method of Achieving Your Personal Objectives

You've already made some fairly extensive and highly useful notes in Chapter 5 on your own needs as you have analyzed them. In this chapter you've converted them into specific objectives and have worked out some plans for achieving them. The time has now come to reality-test these objectives.

The key question here is not whether you want these things. Of course you want them. You wouldn't have listed them if you didn't want them. The important question is: "Do you want them enough to pay the price?" You can get a fix on these questions by honestly laying out the obstacles you see to your reaching each of these objectives.

Take out a sheet of paper and list each of the personal development objectives (Category II objectives) you've planned to achieve. Then list three obstacles you can see to achieving each objective. The obstacles may be maintenance factors on your Category I objectives list, or they may be other blocks to moving ahead. Such blocks as other people, competing responsibilities, or your own lack of prior experience or preparation may be in the way.

Where the barriers are other people and their refusal to remove themselves, you'll have to deal with them through selling skill, consultative skill, or sheer aggression. There'll be more on these techniques later.

Where the barrier is some inadequacy on your part, you may have to add another loop to your plan to make up the deficiency. Take the case of the salesman for an insurance company who wanted to become a claims manager. He had no training. He had a family to support. His boss wasn't eager to see him leave selling where he was

field the person finds his or her choices have been defined. The person may not even consider the possibility of choosing Z, only X and Y are open to him or her.

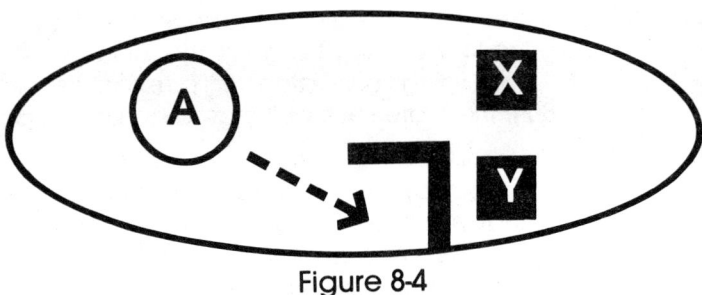

Figure 8-4

Using the salesman as our Person A, we see in Figure 8-4 that the vectors pushing him toward claims work (Y) are being deflected by a barrier whereas the field toward continued selling (X) is open. In resolving his problem, Mr. A must lay out for himself a pattern of the possibles. In this case, because he has a clear path to X and from there can see his way to Y, but cannot go directly to Y, he decides that he will continue selling while he moves from that position into claims work.

This simple scheme probably won't fit you in goal setting, but the general idea will work. Start by defining your goals and laying them out within your own field. Then look at the various factors that affect your field, such as age, financial requirements, family or other responsibilities, education, and the like. These are the factors that are relatively fixed in your case and that you cannot readily find your way around.

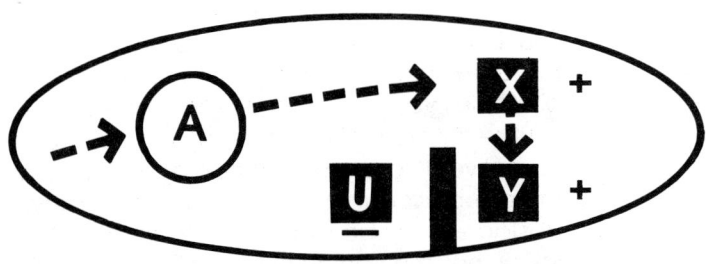

Figure 8-5

The situation to avoid is being cornered and becoming panicky or dismayed. Figure 8-5 shows how you can corner yourself. Mr. A quits his selling job, then finds he can't get a job in claims because he is not qualified. His boss has filled his old spot. This, of course, doesn't make his position impossible, just more complicated. If he had seen his field, rated the vectors pressing him and his goal options, he might have noted that a necessary and perfectly do-able pattern could be worked out. He could stick with selling while he was taking his correspondence course and preparing himself to take the next step, which would be from selling to claims. Thus, selling is not an undesirable option; it is perfectly desirable because it is a necessary step to getting where he really wants to go. He could continue to sell well-perhaps even better-and not be frustrated because he'd know he was making progress.

There might be something new in the field, shown by U, which is a negative goal, or something he wants to avoid at all costs, such as being unemployed. Positive goals are marked with plus signs; negative goals are marked with minus signs.

Can you construct a description of your field, complete with positive and negative goals? Try it.

Chapter 9
Getting Things Done

This chapter deals with a basic approach to personal effectiveness. In some cases, there will be people who report to you; you are their boss. In other cases, there will be people who do work for you, either for pay or because you can persuade them to do things you'd like to have done. Then, there are things **you** must do.

Clearly, you can get more done in this world if you have some help in doing it. When you are in charge of a group of people, or even your own secretary, you can use that available time effectively or ineffectively. Even if you don't supervise anyone on the job, you can practice on your kids at home in organizing your household chores to get them done less laboriously. Then, too, everyone has the chance to practice supervision even before he or she gets promoted to foreman or sales manager on the job. If you belong to a club or church group, you have plenty of opportunities to serve as a member or even as chairman of committees, task forces and work groups.

Every such opportunity can be a learning experience for the person who wishes to study leadership and supervisory practice. There are effective leaders and ineffective ones, and in this chapter we'll be talking about delegation and the effective use of your leadership time and talent to get maximum productivity from other people.

A Systems Approach to Delegation

Several approaches to the control of time are possible for the person who wants to try. (1) You might depend upon "personal efficiency" and drive to cram more activity into each day. (2) You might "push" more work onto others, such as assistants. (3) You might rely upon instruments and forms such as work sheets, pads, calendars and schedules to fit more activity into the available hours. (4) You might take a systems approach, which deals with fundamental efficiency and gets at such basic questions as "Why do it at all?" and "What is the purpose of this activity?"

Here are the basic elements of a system, with some examples of each:

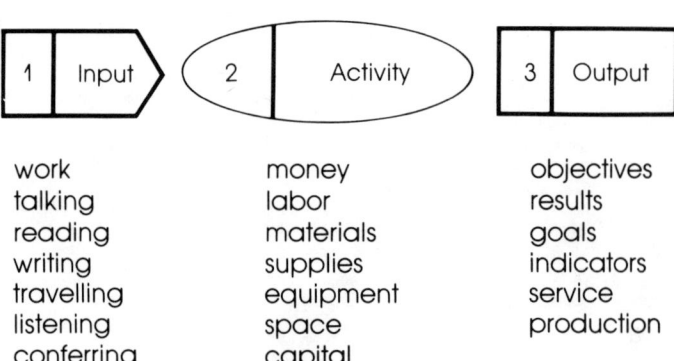

1 Input	2 Activity	3 Output
work	money	objectives
talking	labor	results
reading	materials	goals
writing	supplies	indicators
travelling	equipment	service
listening	space	production
conferring	capital	

- The reason for consuming the **inputs** is to obtain the results.
- The means of achieving the results are **activities.**
- The end results—the consequences—are **outputs.**

The key to the systems approach to delegation is to start with a clear definition of results sought, objectives and output. These should be done in terms of **indicators.** Once the objectives and indicators are clear, agreed to by the boss, the activity can be examined critically and shortcuts to the goals can be worked on. This produces the same output with less time, activity and input.

1. In such a system the person starts with **objectives and results sought,** rather than activity. He or she seeks to control the outputs, first by defining them and, subsequently, by judging all other activity by how well it achieves the indicators of results.

2. The person then turns to the **activities** which are carried out to achieve these objectives and scrutinizes each activity to see if there is a faster, better, easier or cheaper way of getting to the same result—of producing the same or better indicators using fewer inputs.

3. **Inputs and resources** are not released until the first two stages have been completed.

This may appear to be a bit foreign to your customary way of doing things. If so, try it out on your own job. Use the work sheet in Figure 9-1 to define your responsibilities on your present job for the coming year. List these down the left column. Then in the column next to them note the three result ranges you understand to be good performance or bad performance or average expected performance for the coming quarter or year.

If you have any doubts about whether you have picked the right figures, discuss the finished sheet with your boss. This is essential, especially if you are manager, since you will soon be delegating results expected to several other people as their responsibility, and you should be sure that it is right.

Here are some other hints for making your "responsibility results" indicators work as time savers and effectiveness increasers for your own job:

- Start by listing eight to ten major areas of responsibility. List the "trade-offs" when listing these responsibilities. This means that you list those responsibilities which compete with the other responsibilities for your energy. For example, you might be a sales manager or supervisor. You know that dollar volume of sales counts as one area of responsibility. At the same time, you know that gross margin is important and is a trade-off. You might be able to push certain items that have a high price but low margin. This would make your sales volume look great but wouldn't really be a maximum contribution to the business. You might find that in order to maximize gross margin you would have to push certain items in the line that have a lower sales price but that produce a higher gross margin. Examples of other trade-off responsibilities for sales people would include new customers gained, new products introduced, average number of calls made, and average order size.

Goals Work Sheet			
	Output Indicators		
Responsibilities	Pessimistic "minimum acceptable"	Realistic "average"	Optimistic "superior"
1.			
2.			
3.			
4.			
5.			
6.			
7.			
8.			
9.			
10.			

Figure 9-1

- After you've listed your responsibilities as indicated, start identifying your output indicators for each responsibility in the column to the right. Begin with the "average expected" output. This is the realistic amount you are confident can be achieved with good effort. Don't make it a push-over. Last year's average results plus a small improvement might be a normal expected average. Records of past results, share of market sought, or simply organization requirements might be used here.

- List the "maximum probable" outcome in the column to the far right. This would be based on the record-breaking achievements of the past, plus any other ideal outcomes you might hope for. This would be an indicator that you are a superior performer if you achieve this figure. This is the hole-in-one kind of goal, the optimistic goal. Naturally this is what you are really shooting for, but start with reality and work from there. Don't live in a world of illusions but keep the upper target high so that you would really have to stretch to make it.

- List the "lowest possible" outcome that you would dare to permit in the first column to the right of your list of responsibilities. This is the level at which you should notify the boss that something isn't going right. This is the exception point at which you should fire a rocket, wave a red flag, and ask for help. Something has gone sour if you fall below this point in results.

The first stage in the systems approach to delegation then is to define areas of responsibility, establishing indicators of good, average and unsatisfactory as a permissible or possible range. With the responsibilities listed and the range of results defined, you are now able to measure your own performance as you work. You should now know before anybody else whether you are hitting the target or not.

With these objectives and outputs in hand, you can now turn to the next stage, which is controlling your activities–the work you do that produces the results. Remember that the results are what count, and any activity should be judged by how well it contributes to those results and outputs.

Let's look at the second stage in outline form.

    I. **Define your activities.** Use behavioral terms. Remember: Behavior is what you do. "Selling" isn't behavior; what you do is talk, listen, lead a conference. phone, travel, write, dictate, etc.

    II. **Concentrate** on the most time-consuming activities. For sales people this includes travelling, talking, inspecting, interviewing and listening.

    III. **Simplify the activity** by eliminating, combining and changing sequence. Mechanize your manual work (doing dictation, making photocopies, doing computations, etc.). Apply work simplification. Plot work flow studies.

IV. Delegate to others. Delegation is a learning curve, thus you can delegate as fast as you can teach. JIT (Job Instruction Training) speeds training and makes it more certain.

V. Maintain the behavior by controlling favorable and unfavorable consequences, maintaining discipline, and giving situational orders.

In the third stage you plan and release inputs, converting your program into dollars, space and personnel.

Chapter 10
Styles of Leadership

Usually when we think of styles we think of things like the length of women's skirts, the width of men's neckties, new grills on Detroit's latest models, or the "in" choice among Miami beach hotels. What isn't so obvious is that there are styles of leadership that have a definite effect on the skills of the executive. In this chapter we will look at a variety of leadership styles that you might adopt, and we'll consider some options among the various styles which may be relevant to you in your job.

How does your leadership style affect what you do? First, it determines what your policies are like. Second, it determines what kind of people you will recruit. Third, it determines what is included in your training. And, fourth, it determines how you are giong to reward people for achieving things for you.

Styles of leadership have changed about every ten years in my lifetime. Thus it is predictable that the style of leadership that was relevant and prevalent during the 1970s will be modified or even replaced in the 1980s. As economic conditions and personal value systems continue to change we will probably have still another leadership style in the 1990s.

Several leadership styles of the last fifty years are clearly identifiable and are still being practiced today, at least to some extent. That is, some people are trying to manage today with a leadership style that was appropriate to the Twenties or Thirties.

Hard-Nosed Leadership

My first job as a boy was in the mid-Thirties in a Massachusetts textile mill. The all-pervasive leadership style that flourished in those depression years is one which I call the "hard-nose" style. To land my first job I stood in a huge crowd of unemployed outside the shipping dock where a hard-nosed guy in a derby hat came out onto the platform, looked the crowd over, and, for whatever reason, fastening on me said, "You, inside." I shot up the stairs extremely pleased to have that job as so many people were unemployed. When I got inside I found I was working for Hitler's brother. His style was based upon fear of losing a job, fear of having one's income cut off, fearing of being thrown back into that group of unemployed and purposeless people, fear of being dependent on welfare or on someone else.

Work rules reflected the hard-nose style of my textile mill boss. For example, every foreman fired one worker each Friday whether the person deserved to be fired or not. This meant that on Monday the foreman could go back out to the shipping platform to hire one new worker from the group of unemployed assembled there. No one took Monday mornings off because it was clear that if you did you wouldn't have a job on Tuesday. There were no coffee breaks and no Monday morning neuroses. Carrying a newspaper to work was cause for dismissal. In fact, there were dozens of arbitrary, dictatorial grounds for discharge.

Foremen everywhere used fear as a basic motivator. This was the style in textiles where I worked, on the docks, in meat packing plants, and automobile factories. But styles change.

The Human Relations Movement

In 1940, with war clouds gathering and production of war material picking up, the labor force became fully occupied and the leadership style changed.

Picture the foreman the week when the superintendent told him he could not fire anyone on Friday because there were no unemployed persons waiting at the gate outside. Why the man must have been flabbergasted. In fact, it must have been even more dismaying when the superintendent and the personnel manager and other employees at the higher levels began to start telling him he had better be nice to the employees. "Why that is totally unheard of, " he must have exclaimed. "You are watering down the basis of my authority and my leadership."

In many instances the change proved that the foreman was incapable of leadership. He had succeeded in the past by using fear as a system for achieving what he wanted. The old fear-laden, hard-nose style of leadership was dead.

As employees found jobs in ship yards and defense plants, and as employment in consumer goods manufacturing picked up, it became apparent that the kind of supervision that had worked in the Thirties wasn't working anymore. Managers were forced to be more concerned with the satisfaction of their employees at work.

This was the time when the behavioral and social sciences were introduced into the skills of management. Business historians identify this change as the beginning of the human relations movement. . . as the start of the health-and-happiness game.

For, you see, if there was no gang of unemployed eagerly waiting to dash up the stairs and be passive and dependent while immediately doing whatever the boss willed because the boss had something to withhold, then it was apparent that the boss had to adopt a new style. People would quit if they disliked the boss. And if there was no one out on the shipping platform or in the employment office, then such a loss could stop things from being produced. The effect was to handicap the boss.

The ensuing human relations style of leadership was designed to prevent turnover. It aimed at keeping people on the job.

Many of the behavioral scientists of that day found this to be an ample area for research. Psychologists who had previously confined their efforts to studying primates, rabbits, chickens and rats found that managers were a far more lucrative and interesting subject for study. Research at the Hawthorne plant of Western Electric in Chicago, studying what causes people to be productive and creative and to stick with their jobs, became of utmost practical business importance to the corporation.

One of the earliest behavioral science books aimed specifically at managers was "Human Relations in Industry" by Burleigh Gardner. He stated that the objective of the leadership style of the future must be to have contented employees. For, he said, a contented employee is a productive employee. Gardner suggested that contented employees who are happy in their work would be sufficiently grateful to those who provided them with this happiness that they would be productive and creative. Of course, although it is true that a follower must be contented to be productive, there are as many unproductive followers who are even more contented. This, we were to discover in the late Fifties, was inflationary.

Management By Pressure

The human relations movement of the Forties and early Fifties was found to have a number of undersirable side effects. Chief among these was that it taught people to be discontented. A Harvard professor identified the problem noting that most of the effect of the human relations movement during that period of time was to teach people to pick at the scabs of their emotions.

Results were another disappointment. One large medical supply manufacturer in New Jersey brought in a survey research team from the University of Chicago to study employee morale. The researchers found morale to be low. So a major program was initiated to improve morale by providing nice things for nice people, by offering all sorts of extra benefits, and by selecting pleasant and deferential bosses who would let employees do anything they wanted to do. A year later the group was restudied by the same research team. Morale was found to have increased by twenty points. . . but production had fallen fifteen per cent!

Clearly, a peg is needed upon which to hang the human relations thing. Perhaps it is found by answering the question, "What are we in business for?" or "Why does this organization exist?" Is it to make workers happy, or is it to produce goods and services that other people want and are willing to pay for as consumers or as taxpayers?

We faced a dilemma. We couldn't go back to the "good old days" when the leader was the boss (an authoritarian) who ruled by fear. And we found that the health-and-happiness days of building a country club atmosphere not only didn't yield a productive gratitude but made people increasingly concerned with what more the employer could do for them.

What emerged was a compromise between the health-and-happiness and the hard-nose leadership styles. This compromise might be identified as "management by pressure." The big wheel at the top makes a quarter turn and the little wheel at the bottom makes thirty-two revolutions just by the distance it is from the energizing force. Management by pressure sought to produce anxiety in the hope that the psychological pressure would force people to be more successful. But management by pressure was short-lived. It was soon replaced by situational management, which is the leadership style today.

Situational Management

Situational management is as rooted in the environment as is the manager. Some common behavior patterns of situational managers are that they know where they are and what kind of environment they are able to relate to the followers near them.

Situational management will be looked at more closely in the next chapter. What I'd like you to consider at this point is that leadership styles have changed precisely because the environment has changed. Note that the depression environment of the Thirties produced a possibility of a style of management that was quite easy to execute. Management by fear was made possible by the dependency of the followers–a job was extremely valuable and money was scarce. The terror of the depression with one of every four workers being unemployed made it possible to use an authoritarian style.

A condition of labor shortage, however, necessitated a different employer-employee relationship. One simply could no longer get away with management by fear if employers needed workers more than the worker needed the employer.

But the environment is more complex than this. The work force of the Twenties and Thirties was less educated the that of today. The person who had completed no school whatsoever was employable at the end of World War I if he or she had sufficient ability to mark an "X" on a piece of paper indicating receipt of the pay envelope. This had changed by the late Thirties when a high school education became a requirement for employment. But along with the diploma some new values were acquired. Among the information extracted from the study of history, social science, government, and maybe some psychology and economics, was knowledge of the dignity of man and of the right of people to have some say in the decisions affecting them. This became particularly true as the educational level advanced to college.

Only one out of every two hundred employees was an engineer in 1920, but by 1950 one out of every nineteen employees in large corporations was an engineer. Engineers and other professionals (accountants, lawyers, actuaries, metallurgists, sales managers, etc.) are technical and managerial persons with professional skills and middle class values. They expect people who haven't acquired their technical skills, including bosses (whatever their rank), will listen to their opinions on the decisions affecting them, especially in those areas in which they have been professionally trained.

The gap between bosses who went to work in the 1930s and a new generation of young employees became explosive in the late Sixties and early Seventies. The bosses had acquired their orientation as to what the behavior should be from the bosses they had worked under in the Thirties. When they tried to apply management by fear under the guise of management by pressure they encountered opposition and rebellion.

Meanwhile, teachers and managers began to discover that the articles of faith for learning in one decade how to be a leader in another was poor training. The situational manager found that past experience didn't necessarily apply to present situations, and that the skills developed in the past may need to be changed again and again over periods of time as one's relationship with his or her followers and their value systems change.

Full employment, the rise of professionals, and changing value systems all combined to create a new environment.

The element of leadership style that distinguishes the situational manager from his and her predecessors is that situational managers lead through the abilities of their followers, not through their own personal abilities and intuitions. A supervisor who says he or she is surrounded by pipsqueaks should be asked who hired and trained them, who tells them what is expected, and who tells them how well (or poorly) they are doing. A leader whose followers are pipsqueaks is the chief pipsqueak.

> **The performance of a leader is measured by the quality and performance of his or her followers.**

Situational leadership demands that the leader be able to relate to the environment in order to control, predict and shape it. The situational leader is more apt to be a manager of a decision making machine that to be an individual decision maker.

Leading the New Generation

Young professionals comprise a new element in the environment which will necessitate new changes in leadership style. Any new leadership style that you develop to manage the new generation will have to be based on their value system. They want to know the basic purposes of the organization. They are unwilling to accept meaningless activity. They want meaning and relevance and being where the action is. They want to do important work. They want to arrive at self-actualization and self-expression.

> **Stated simply, the new leadership style for the 1980s and on into the 1990s must be more goal oriented and less activity centered.**

Youngsters today are willing to pursue worthwhile goals and they are willing to expend the time and effort needed to seek achievement at a very high level. However, they will not accept the absurdity of activity for its own sake. The kind of bureaucratic procedures ably described in Joseph Heller's novel "Catch-22" are offensive to the new generation.

What does this new generation expect from its leaders?

1. They want meaningful objectives.
2. They want to know how well they are doing in their work while they are doing it.
3. They want to know how well they did when the whole process is completed.
4. They expect that their recognition for success (including pay and promotion and other forms of recognition) be for results, rather than for conformity or pointless activity.

Figures from the U.S. Department of Labor indicate there will be a shortage of people in the thirty-to-forty-year-old age bracket from which most managers are selected. As a result, we will have to dip into a younger group to find people who can staff all the supervisory, professional, project management and key staff positions that will be required in our expanding economy with growing companies and in society at large. In effect, the talent shortage says that unless our leadership style can manage the new generation effectively we can expect tremendous competitive disadvantages in our individual organizations.

Today's young person asks: "What must I do to get ahead around here?" "How do they pick the people they choose to promote?" "Does anybody up there know what I want to do? Do they know what I can do? Do they even know what I am doing?"

The major criteria by which the new generation feels people should be judged is that of whether the person set high goals, and aspired to achieve great things; solve problems, and be innovative and creative. In addition, the new generation employee wants to know whether managers reward those things when they see them.

To manage the new generation effectively you've got to to hang up some exciting purposes before people. Telling them where they're going is not enough. Each young person should be presented a goal and be required to plan to achieve it.

Chapter 11
Situational Management

As noted earlier, sometimes explanations of behavior can be found inside the individual who acts in a certain way. In other cases the explanation isn't found inside but is found in the outside environment. Let's call this the "situation." Understanding how we are affected by the environment arms us to make changes in that environment to affect our own behavior. If we find ourselves in an intolerable situation, and, as a result, we behave badly, we should probably move elsewhere.

Understanding also helps us to predict and control the behavior of others. When we note that others behave badly or well in a certain kind of environment, we may be able to "correct their behavior" by altering the situation or by changing the stimuli which press them into acting a certain way.

Match Behavior To The Situation

To clarify this principle of situational management let's start with you and some of your own behavior. There are probably some things you do which you regret, or which you hope to correct. Perhaps you make foolish errors under certain circumstances, or perhaps you show your worst side under certain conditons.

Try noting on a sheet of paper some of the situations in which your behavior displeases you, makes you mad at yourself or gets you into troubles that you'd like to avoid. In the first column make a list of those types of behavior that you'd like to eradicate. Then, in the second column, list the kinds of environment, conditions, people, or situations that seem to be associated with that behavior. The example given in Figure 11-1 obviously doesn't fit your behavior (now that you've outgrown youthfulness), but it is useful in several ways: (1) It shows how specific kinds of stimuli of general nature can affect our behavior. (2) it gives you a cue about watching for signs of unusual or undesirable behavior, and about identifying the situational forces that apparently trigger such behavior. (3) It sets up a warning system. If John were to be reflective about his own behavior (and desired to change it), he might tell himself something like this: "Oh, oh! Another substitute teacher. I'd better be cool or I'll be in hot water with the floor master again." (4) It

Behavioral action	Kinds of environment or situational surroundings in which you do these things
1. Young John Smith, usually well-behaved, acts foolishly and shows off, talks loudly, engages in horse play, and makes a general nuisance of himself.	1. Whenever he is with older boys. 2. Whenever there is a substitute teacher. 3. Whenever girls are around.

Figure 11-1

gives some hints to his superiors about controlling his behavior, since they will be able to set up some controls or counter-forces when they know that the triggering situation will be occurring. (5) John can be taught to recognize the cause and effect relationship which apparently exists between such situations and his behavior.

What are some of the triggering situations for you, and what kinds of behavior do they bring about? For example, you might find the relationships listed in Figure 11-2 as being common in people with behavioral problems. The triggers mentioned here are varied in type, just as they are in real life. Sometimes we overlook some of the stimuli because the connection doesn't seem obvious. Something like a sales contest, a bonus plan, or a merit system for making pay raises are triggers. They are the "created triggers," but they certainly aren't the only kind, or even the most important kind.

Trigger	Behavior
Jim drinks two martinis at noon.	Jim Smith talks too much.
A customer insults his product.	Jim Smith insults the customer personally.
Somebody calls Jim a "peddler"	Jim sulks and doesn't speak to the person.
Triggers can also be favorable in their effect	
A sales contest is announced.	Jim works an hour extra every day.
A customer praises his product.	Jim responds with flattery and sincere appreciation.

Figure 11-2

The System As A Trigger To Behavior

We all live in a world of systems. Being rational, human beings like to arrange matters so that they have a flow, a sequence, a beginning, a middle, and an end. When we arrange matters systematically, many unpredicted triggers to behavior emerge.

An example is the engineering department where many engineers failed to turn their reports in on time. At first the manager considered this to be a personality defect in the engineers; then he thought it might be a motivation problem, but finally, after an analysis of triggers in the system, he found these conditions existed: (1) It was impossible to find a quiet place to write. (2) Typewriters weren't available. (3) There was a shortage of secretarial help. (4) Proper supplies were not easily obtained. After taking action to eliminate all these situational factors reports began to come in on time.

At the Massachusetts Institute of Technology's library it was found desirable to have students needing assistance from the librarian sit down during such sessions in order that a more intelligent discussion be conducted. Signs advising people to "be seated" had little effect, but by reconstructing the counter and lowering it the physical setting was arranged in such a way that the student was obliged to sit on a low stool to get the attention of the library assistant on duty. Shortly everyone was being seated while explaining his or her needs to the library staff person.

Another example is that of the safety-preaching plant supervisor who found that he was most effective in preventing accidents when he wired the guards so the drive motor of the machine stopped automatically whenever the guard was lifted.

You could undoubtedly construct a few examples of your own if you tried.

The Advantages of Situational Management

There are at least six benefits gained in human relation by attacking behavior change situationally as the first step.

1. You'll find that the situational change generates less human resistance, since people don't resist situations as much as they do personal orders. Take the case of the husband who always started an argument when his wife told him to wear his galoshes on rainy days. She finally solved this situationally. When it looked rainy, she placed his rubbers in the doorway through which he left every morning. She then wisely stayed out of sight. Finding it foolish to argue with the mute rubbers sitting there, he often put them on since they, rather than his wife, were "ordering" him to do so.

2. The behavior is more likely to change if the situation seems to issue the orders rather than the boss. For one thing, the boss is apt to forget, to say something in the wrong tone of voice, and perhaps to end up with a dispute. The dispute then becomes more important than the desired behavior.

3. The best orders are those that appear to be given by the situation. A duty roster posted to show who is on some onerous detail seems to be presenting some systematic fact rather then the arbitrary whim of an individual leader. Rather then saying, "The lunch hour phone duty will be the responsibility of Marc today," the boss has a chart showing rotation and before lunch asks clearly: "Who is next on the lunchtime duty chart?" At this point, if Marc wants to argue, he is in effect arguing with a chart which is, of course, a foolish thing to do. The boss can rightly say, " I didn't pick you to stay late; the chart did it."

4. When verbal instructions are given, they may be made to seem situational by the manner in which they are stated. Rather than the foreman saying to Harry, 'Hey, Harry, drop that carton and carry this shovel over there," he might achieve the same effect without raising anybody's hackles by presenting the change as a changed situation: "Harry, we've got a hot job that I've just noticed. This shovel has to go across the yard. The carton can wait until after you've finished the first job." Note that the shovel has suddenly made up its mind that it wants to be carried elsewhere. Thus, when handled as a situational matter rather than a personal master-and-slave relationsip, the whole incident becomes more objective. In Figure 11-3 write down a few orders you might give or receive, and see if you can convert them into situation forms.

The Personal Order	The Situational Order
"Go wash those windows"	"Those windows could stand a good washing today"
_____	_____
_____	_____
_____	_____

Figure 11-3

5. Accentuate the positive. There's plenty of research evidence to show that positive orders or instructions will get a more favorable response than negative or avoidance orders. The boss who tells subordinates, " Don't go outside the yellow lines or you'll be subject to discharge," will find that a positive statement will be more effective and will bring better compliance and acceptance. " Stay inside the yellow lines at all times. This is an important rule for your own safety. " With a little thought and practice you'll be able to say things in a positive way rather than a negative one. Use Figure 11-4 as a work chart to practice wording a few of your common directives or orders that could be stated positively rather than negatively. After you note the example, fill in your own examples.

Negative Order	Positive Version
"Keep off the grass."	"Please stay on the sidewalk at all times."
_____	_____
_____	_____
_____	_____

Figure 11-4

6. Avoid ultimatums and threats in orders. In addition to turning the orders into positive situational expressions, avoid the "or else" tail to any order. "Please don't file salmon colored copies. Offenders will be disciplined" is an example of an order which will probably arouse resentment even in the best worker and, in all likelihood, won't deter the chronic offender from violating the rule or disobeying the order. The ultimatum–or punishment-tail–at the end of an order is a pointed gun, aimed at random to reflect some doubt about the

order giver's ability to get things done because they are right. It is a naked use of power and dictatorship. Then, too, it implies that if anyone fails, punishment must be applied. If it isn't, the boss loses effectiveness in those instances where actual disciplinary action is required.

Discipline as Situational Behavior Change

In those cases where some flagrant violation of rules and regulations has occurred and discipline is called for, the situational approach is equally useful. Following are the conditions necessary to make situational discipline work:

First, eliminate the offense; don't punish the offender. The purpose is not to exact retributive justice but to assure correct behavior in the future.

Second, be sure the rules are known and communicated to everyone affected and are applied equally to all persons.

Third, have a successively more severe kind of sanction which is applied for successive offenses. Start with:

- instruction in the right way and warning not to repeat the offenses;
- for second offenses, repetition of the instructions and reprimand of the offender;
- for third offenses, some kind of punitive action, such as temporary layoff of several days or one week without pay;
- for further repetition fo offenses, discharge.

By adhering to this sort of system all of the requirements of fairness, as well as defensibility of your action, are met. Labor arbitrators have repeatedly upheld all of these stages, if they have been impartially applied.

- Always make notes of the actions taken and file them.
- Don't carry earlier offenses over for more than a year. At the end of a year following the first offense, clear the slate.
- Never discipline when angry.
- Discipline in private, not in front of the offender's colleagues.
- Never touch a person physically during the disciplinary process (you might get punched in the eye).
- Never use abusive language or profanity in the disciplinary process, even when it may be the customary language of the shop.
- Above all, make sure offenders know they have entered a four-stage process when they are at the first step. This explains the situation to them.

In practice, such an orderly system, well managed, will prevent most wrong behavior and will correct it when it appears.

Chapter 12
Using Your Time Effectively

Without objectives there can be no effectiveness. The word "effective" implies action as a contributing force in objectives. Thus, with your objectives in hand on your own job, you can now proceed to sharpen your own effectiveness in the knowledge that the essential preliminary step is out of the way. Furthermore, you have these job objectives in a form that makes it possible for you to tell whether the results are poor, good or excellent.

Your yardstick for every activity from here on as you go about your job is the set of objectives you have defined. You have criteria for judging your own effectiveness.

The second stage of your system for getting action involves looking at your personal effectiveness and determining how it can be improved. Five steps are included here:
- Define your activities.
- Concentrate on the most time-consuming activity.
- Simplify the activity.
- Delegate to others.
- Maintain the behavior.

Let's look at each in some detail.

Define Your Own Activity

The hardest discipline in defining your activity is avoiding terms that are too general. Remember that behavior is what you **do**. You should stick to things that are specific actions on your part.
- Start by preparing a "time analyzer." Keep a running log of how you actually spend your day. This will take less time than you'd suspect and will pay off handsomely in time saved in the long pull. Keep it up for ten days, then move to the next step. The ten days don't have to be consecutive; they can be randomly spread through a month.
- Examine these activities critically by asking, "How did I use my time?"
- Measure your activities against the results achieved for what you did by asking, "Did this activity make a significant contribution to my objectives?"

Most people who have any kind of managerial staff or professional tasks have some devices at hand to help them manage their time. A calendar pad is the basic tool used by most people, yet this could be more useful than it is. You might arrange it in a format that helps you analyze your time at the same time your schedule is being planned and executed.

The time analyzer in Figure 12-1 can do this for you. It's just a variation of your desk calendar. If you have an office copier at hand you can prepare a couple dozen of these and use them at your desk in lieu of a regular calendar. You'll note that it has three major parts:
- The "make ready and plan" segment shows what your plans and appointments are in additon to tasks outlined.

Personal Effectiveness / 75

DAILY SCHEDULE AND TIME ANALYZER   Date:_____

Make Ready and Plan			Do	Analysis
Hours	Actual Work Hours	Appointment or Tasks Planned	Specific Accomplishments	Comments
1				
2				
3				
4				
5				
6				
7				
8				

Figure 12-1

- The "do" segments for making notations on what you actually accomplished against what you planned. Perhaps you planned to do more than was humanly possible, or perhaps you let distractions chew up your time.
- The "analysis" segment is for analyzing how you used your time.

By keeping your day's work planned thus, you are also setting up your activity in a way that makes it easy to analyze the activities of a dozen or more days in retrospect. You simply collect the sheets for that many days and take them home and summarize them. This helps you see areas for cutting out extra steps and unnecessary efforts.

How do you analyze how you use your time? Here are ten techniques supervisors can use to organize their time efficiently and cut down on wasted time.

(1) List all you job duties. Jot down your daily tasks, plus others that come up periodically or irregularly. Arrange duties in order of importance–first things first.

(2) Figure the time required for each. Estimate the amount of time required to handle each duty properly. The major tasks–not minor ones–should be assigned the most time.

(3) Make a timetable for the week. Plan next week's work this week. List what you expect to accomplish each day. Leave some periods open for thinking, planning, and unexpected developments.

(4) Cross off activities as you finish them. Actually use the timetable. Keep it as a guide–it will show your daily progress. Save it as a record of your work.

(5) Review and revise your timetable every night. Take inventory in the last few minutes of every workday, then plan your next day's work. Revise the timetable as needed, and keep it flexible.

(6) Delegate work to subordinates. Study your list of job duties. Ask yourself: "What work can I assign to my subordinates?" The leader should organize, delegate and supervise.

(7) Train subordinates to handle more of your tasks. Develop them to handle new tasks. Teach them. This then marks you as a good trainer and results in more time for planning and thinking.

(8) Streamline your meetings and conversations. Ask yourself: "Am I spending too much time in idle conversation, interviews and meetings?" Train yourself and others to "get to the point" without sacrificing friendliness.

(9) Control the time you spend on the telephone. Perhaps someone can screen your incoming calls and place your outgoing calls. How many are really necessary? Can some be delegated? Can you make yourself "unavailable" during certain hours?

(10) Increase your reading speed. Find out how fast you can read. Library books and courses are available to help you speed up your reading. Will power and concentration can raise your reading speed to four hundred words a minute.

The kind of calendar you employ may be useful to you in another way. Since you are giving of yourself when you give of your time, you should be austere in how you spend it. Planning whole days may be uneconomical, and planning fragments of days will become an important aspect of managing your time.

The lawyer is taught in law school to manage his or her time through use of a diary, in which every hour of professional effort is to be charged off against one case or another for purposes of billing. This same principle is worth trying if you want to be professional in the management of your time.

Calendars that display a whole month of days at a time have a useful effect in managing a whole month. They are available in all stationery stores. Such a calendar assists you in scheduling events ahead, and it is useful for looking back to discover where your "unbilled hours" went.

You can not only display your own personal time, but also other significant events which can affect you. You might note deadlines, and, since they are displayed in one broad scope, you can see them before they creep up on you and precipitate a crisis that could have been averted.

As an aside, we might note that crises are often–perhaps most often–the creation of the people who are caught in them. This may seem strange, but many people apparently enjoy crises and unconsciously create them for the attention and furor that will ensue. This is simply ineffective performance. The person who seems to have the most time is often merely the one who rigidly plans it.

Cast a Cold Eye at Your Results

As you can see if you've tried this for a day or two, logging accurate and complete information isn't really much of a chore if you use the analyzer type of daily calendar plus a monthly visual display calendar. You are doing most of the things required to generate this useful information already, it is merely that you are now displaying it in a more useful fashion at the same time you are generating it.

The next step is to take a couple of hours to improve the use of the time based upon analysis of the data. Professor Earl Brooks of Cornell University has prescribed a five-step plan for corporate executives for doing just that. You can try it on your own if you have the information at hand. The five steps can be listed as follows:

1. Develop information on how you are using your time.
2. Question every item for each expenditure of time.
3. Develop an improved schedule for the immediate future.
4. Develop better methods of doing the same tasks.
5. Apply your improved plan.

After trying this first go-round on your own work, re-do the process and improve it again. When you are convinced that you have found more time and are working more effectively, you'll find that there is more of your energy going toward results and less lost in backtracking, duplication and unproductive work.

Let's look at each of these in outline form.

Improving the Use of Your Time

I. How are you using your time?
  A. Analyze the demands on your time.
     1. What are you doing? List for a week or a month.
     2. Classify your time expenditures as:
        a. Regular or recurring–keeping the wheels turning;
        b. Emergency or problem solving–putting out fires;
        c. Developmental or creative–making significant long-term improvements.
  B. What else should you be doing?
  C. What are you doing that could be eliminated, modified or delegated?

II. For each expenditure of time, question:
  A. Why is it necessary?
  B. What is its essential purpose?
  C. When should it be done? What's its priority?
  D. Who should do it?
  E. Where should it be done?
  F. How should it be done?

III. Develop improved schedule to:
  A. Eliminate unnecessary or low priority functions;
  B. Delegate or assign to others;
  C. Combine jobs and places.

IV. Develop even better methods.
  A. How efficient are your methods of management in:
     1. Developing plans?
     2. Establishing objectives and standards?
     3. Developing people?
     4. Making decisions?
     5. Communicating in:
        a. Interviews and discussions;
        b. Writing;
        c. Reading;
        d. Meetings;
        e. Telephoning;
        f. Travel?
     6. Relationships with others?
     7. Reviewing and measuring results?
  B. What more can your secretary do to help you improve your management effectiveness?

V. Apply your improved plan.
  A. Review your methods and results.
  B. Re-plan for:
     1. Projects;
     2. Time;
     3. People.
  C. Rearrange your plan.

D. Spend more time on developmental and creative projects.
E. Develop standards of performance (define results expected).
F. Work out ideas with others:
  1. Superior.
  2. Subordinates.
  3. Staff and associates.

Did the Activity Pay Off?

The final test of your activity isn't whether or not you did it faster. The whole idea isn't to speed you but to make the actions you took more effective.

In order to do this you must assess whether or not your behavior had consequences which were favorable or unfavorable in terms of the contribution to objectives.

Remember that action alone isn't good; it should have favorable consequences most of the time, or at least more often than it has unfavorable consequences in terms of results.

Some of your most vigorous and efficient activities might be carrying you toward the wrong goal, in which case the effects are on the negative side. A German general once said that we should "beware the man who is stupid and energetic." This doesn't fit you, of course, but the effect is the same if you aren't careful to note the consequences of your actions. The best way here is to note what your objectives are, then take a sample of some of your behavior. You needn't log this while it is going on. In fact, it will be best done by recalling some of the actions you took and then honestly appraising what happened as a result of your behavior.

Did Your Efforts Make Things Happen?

Figure 12-2 is illustrative of how this works. In the left hand column are lists of possible activities and behavior in which you might have engaged. Go over the list and see if you did any of these things. In the column to the right note what others did as a result of your behavior. In the last column mark a plus sign (+) for those consequences that were favorable; that is, the results contributed to your objectives. Mark a minus sign (-) for unfavorable outcomes and a zero (0) for neutral. If you can't tell whether an action contributed toward your objectives, write a question mark (?).

In studying the consequences of your behavior, note the following:

- You must have your own objectives in mind before you start to simplify your own activity.
- You must have some indication of whether your boss approves your responsibilities before you delegate to others.
- When you delegate to others you will delegate responsibilities as defined by indicators, rather than work to be done.

- Realism at all times is most important. Don't play games of self-deception and self-delusion. "Next year we're going to produce double the volume of this year" may be a laudable statement, but unless you have a plan for getting there it's a way of getting yourself trapped into a disappointing year-end letdown. You can make improvements if you face up to reality; and improvement, not perfections, is the essence of reality.

Your action	Check here if applies	What others did as a result of your action	Gain Loss
Example: Bawled out secretary	X	Started crying–lost 2 hours	–
Example: Told a man he was doing job wrong	X	He corrected his method and eliminated spoilage	+
1. Watched employee work.			
2. Led employee meeting.			
3. Signed production or sales report.			
4. Signed requisition.			
5. Talked with other supervisor.			
6. Drank coffee and talked with men.			
7. Talked to mechanic about breakdown.			
8. Read a micrometer.			
9. Talked to salesman on the phone.			
10. Wrote a quality complaint report.			
11. Soothed a mad union steward.			
12. Walked into boss's office.			
13. Make vacation schedule.			
14. Talked to good-looking female employee.			
15. Read **Wall Street Journal.**			

Your action	Check here if applies	What others did as a result of your action	Gain Loss
17. Walked with a box of product in hand.			
18. Drew on graph paper.			
19. Studied blue-print.			
20. Read first proofs of advertisement.			
21. Put papers in briefcase.			
22. Had conversation with boss.			
23. Gave worker a break—took his place on the job.			
24. Helped one of your salesmen close the big deal.			
25. Operated slide rule.			
26. Wrote minutes of a meeting.			
27. Told your secretary about her typing errors.			
28. Drew a flow chart of work.			
29. Read seniority list.			
30. Drove company car.			
31. Soothed irate employee.			
32. Sat and thought about next year.			
33. Had a "How am I doing?" talk with subordinate.			
34. Explained a job to employee.			
35. Took inventory of parts in stock.			
36. Read a meter.			
37. Talked to employee about a transfer.			
38. Listened to a "tattle tale."			

Your action	Check here if applies	What others did as a result of your action	Gain Loss
39. Made small talk with union president.			
40. Listened to two angry employees with differences.			
41. Told new employee how to find the lounge.			
42. Conducted safety inspection.			
43. Signed leave of absence papers.			
44. Designed a new form.			
45. Talked to a job candidate.			
46. Asked employee's opinion.			
47. Read a management book.			
48. Praised a man for good work.			
49. Discharged an incompetent person.			
50. Worked overtime.			
(List others of your own)			
51.			
52.			
53.			
54.			
55.			
56.			
57.			
58.			
59.			
60.			
61.			

Figure 12-2

Chapter 13
Simplifying the Job—Working Smarter, Not Harder

Having turned your attention inward upon yourself and your own activities, you can now turn your attention outward to the details of the job itself. You'll recall that in Chapter Nine we detailed a three-stage plan for improving your personal effectiveness. The first step was defining objectives. The second was studying each activity to see how much it contributed to those objectives. (If it makes no contribution, toss it out.) The same plan of attack you used on your personal work patterns can be used on the work itself.

> **It is necessary to study the work itself because (1) you might be very efficient in doing something that shouldn't be done in the first place, (2) you might be doing something twice, and (3) you might be cancelling out one hour's work during the next hour.**

We'll be drawing on some well-known principles of industrial engineering in order to simplify work, but you don't have to be an engineer to use them. Though these are merely organized common sense, they do follow the engineer's method of attacking problems methodically and systematically.

A Six-Step Plan for Simplifying Your Job

Before your start simplifying you job, remember that your aren't going to cut out anything that produces a necassary result. You may not be permitted to short-cut things (such as checks, audits, reports, or other essentials) where those steps produce results that somebody wants. The idea isn't to get you to speed up, nor is it to reduce the results, but to get the same results more easily by concentrating on the way you are doing the job. However, instead of concentrating on your own activity, as we did in the previous chapter, we'll concentrate on the job itself.

Here's a six-step plan for simplifying your job:

Step 1–Pick a job to study for improvement.
Step 2–List the objectives of the job in terms of results.
Step 3–List the present details of the job.
Step 4–Question every detail of the job for its contribution to objectives and for relative costs.
Step 5–Develop a new method for doing the job to achieve the same objectives.
Step 6–Install the new method and check it periodically.

Each step will be examined in turn.

Pick a Job to Study for Improvement

Your first impulse may be to think that any job that has been in existence for a long period of time is probably being done in the most effective possible way. Nevertheless, even those jobs that were set up by detailed engineering study can lend themselves to improvement if we turn a questioning mind upon them. Clearly some jobs suggest themselves as being loaded with more fat and waste than others, and here would be the best place to start. You should realize, however, that no job is being done in the best way, and that the way in which every job is being done can be improved upon!

Here are some hints on picking a job to simplify:

- Pick one with which your boss has expressed discontent.
- Pick one which takes up most of your time in repetitive work.
- Pick one which is a bottleneck, that is, one that seems to be holding up other jobs because it is slower.
- Pick a job where trouble and delay seem to cluster.

You pick a job in such a way that you can study it for improvement. That is, you define a "job" as a repetitive cycle of tasks, or a series of flow paths of a form, a part, or a person. Stick to one item, person, or task at a time, and then proceed to another facet of the job.

List the Objectives of the Job in Terms of Results

After you've named the job you intend to study for simplifying, move on to listing the objectives of that job. The main idea here is to eliminate the whole job if possible. There's no point in charting and studying something that isn't needed any more. The tendency to hang onto things no longer required is far too common.

- List the results that occur because the job is being done.
- If the above seems difficult, try listing the effects if the job were eliminated.
- If the objectives aren't apparent to you, check with others. If, for example, you are routinely filling out a form, check to see if the user really needs it and wants it continued. Also ask your boss, "What is the purpose of this job?"
- Put this objective down in writing before you start eliminating details. Keep it handy.

List All the Details

The entire process should be diagrammed and written out on a piece of paper when you are defining the details of a job. A sample of such a process chart on what you do when signing a letter is shown in Figure 13-1. First, list every step in the process, showing distances, times, weights, and giving a graphic picture of every step. A map-like sketch of the work place layout and a series of numbered lines tracing each step from place to place, showing times required, often points up some obvious inefficiencies. The process chart can use symbols to reveal graphically exactly what is happening at each stage of the process.

Now, of course, the idea of a process chart on signing a letter isn't intended to teach you how to sign a letter but to illustrate the principle of getting all of the details. You'll usually find that simple hand work can be further simplified and improved only if it is frequently repeated. If

Process chart-Signing a Letter		
Step	Time in Seconds	Distance in Inches
1. Reach for pen		
2. Grasp pen		
3. Transport pen to paper		
4. Sign name to letter		
5. Transport pen to holder		
6. Release pen		
7. Return hand to original position		

Figure 13-1

you take such a job and study it you'll come up with results that look like those found in a study of a collating operation in an office (Figure 13-2).

How was this result achieved? In the old method the secretary laid the twelve pages to be collated around the edge of a table and walked around picking up a sheet at a time. These were then stacked, and she continued around the table like a horse operating a circular water pump. In the second method a rack was constructed with the numbered sheets in one of each slots in the rack. The rack was placed within arms' reach of the secretary so she could do the job while seated by just reaching out, using both hands at once. The result was a new method.

Not only were time and motion saved, but fatigue was reduced and the job was completed almost seven minutes sooner thus allowing her time to get on to other things without having worked one bit harder.

	Old	Improved	Saved
Total number of operations	38	14	24
Total distance travelled (walked)	13,000 ft.	stationary	13,000
Total time per 1000 sheets	12.4 min.	5.8 min.	6.6 min.

Figure 13-2

Question Every Detail of the Job

Once you have defined every detail of the job, you then question every detail.

Why is it necessary?	Could it be eliminated?
What is its purpose?	Is the present method fixed?
When should it be done?	Could you change the sequence?
Who should do it?	Could another person do it more easily?
Where should it be done?	Could a better location help?
How should it be done?	Is there a better way?

With the answers to the above questions you are then in a position to apply some tested principles of motion economy as they relate to human activity.

1. Working with two hands at once is better than working with only one hand, or one hand at a time.
2. When both hands are used, they should start and finish their motions together to obtain rhythm.
3. Motions of the arms should be made in opposite and symmetrical directions, not in the same direction; and they should be made simultaneously. This cuts fatigue.
4. Eye movements should be planned to permit as few eye fixations as possible. This means that you bunch together things to be done rather than spread them out.
5. Try to keep the number of hand motions as low as possible. This means that the order of preference is as follows:
    - Finger motions alone are best.
    - Motions involving fingers and wrist are next best.
    - Motions involving fingers, wrists, forearm and upper arm are next best.
    - Motions involving all of the above plus shoulder and body are least efficient.
6. Use gravity to deliver materials rather than "carrying down" the work. This means you may devise chutes and slides in preference to using human energy where gravity can do the work.
7. Continued curved motion is less fatiguing than sudden sharp changes in direction.
8. Always try to arrange the work so that rhythm can be built into the activity being performed.
9. When tools or devices are used, always have a fixed station where they are located. This is also true of materials. If workers must look each time they want to use something, time is lost. Workers should be able to find each tool or each material without looking.
10. Locate all of the tools, parts and supplies within arms' reach of the worker if possible.
11. Any materials which are to be used should be fed to the worker by gravity feed bins, trays or chutes where possible.
12. Locate materials, tools and supplies to permit the best sequence of

the work to be done. You'll note in Figure 13-3 on the collating example cited above that the trays are arranged so that the secretary reaches to the outside extremities of the trays for sheets 1 and 2, then down one level at the same range for 3 and 4.

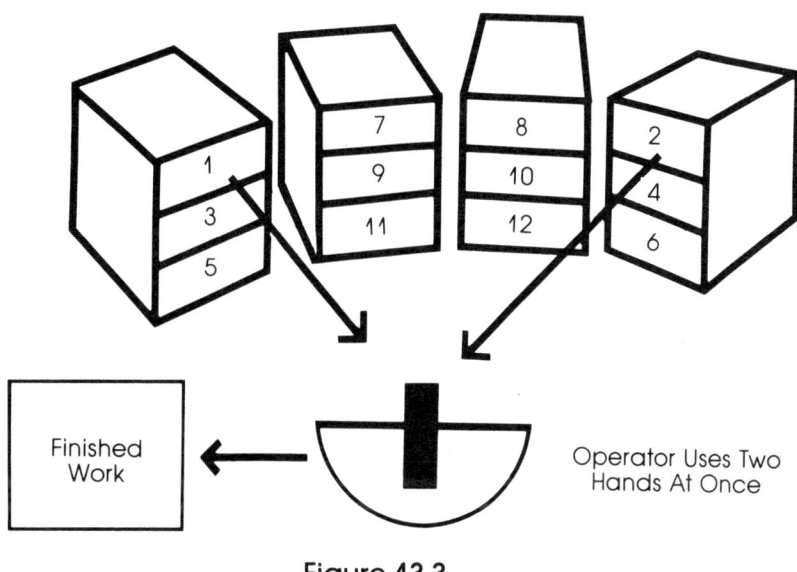

Figure 13-3

13. Work done sitting down is preferable to work done standing or walking.
14. Lighting should be adequate to prevent eye fatigue and errors.
15. The seating arrangement should permit alternate sitting and standing to relieve monotony and fatigue.
16. A posture-preserving chair should be provided for work done while seated.
17. The hands should be relieved of work that can be done by other parts of the body. Knee levers, foot pedals and similar devices can add to output without speeding up the hands.
18. If tools are used, combining two or more into a single one will reduce the activity required. Pencils with erasers on the end are an example.
19. If finger work is involved, distribute the work over all of the fingers equally. The hunt-and-peck typist never can beat the trained ten-finger typist.
20. The most economical way of transporting things is not transporting them. Transportation adds nothing but time and cost to the job.
21. Where the hand is used to perform a task, any handles or knobs should permit as much of the surface of the hand to come in contact with the handles or knobs as possible.
22. Switches, knobs and levers should be placed close enough to the workers so they can reach them without leaving their work stations.

23. In stacking materials, supplies and books, vertical stacking (as with library books) is more efficient than horizontal stacking (like the layers of a cake). Individual units can be removed and replaced this way without moving all of the stack.
24. Work should be planned to follow a cyclical pattern with a beginning, a middle and an end wherever possible. This permits estimates of standard times and shortens learning time.

Develop a New Method

If you have followed these steps, by this time you have undoubtedly noted many areas of potential improvement. Next to your diagram or charting of your old method, answer each critical and analytical question with a proposed simplification or new method. Keep track of the old method and the new method and note any savings which have occurred.

Install the New Method

Before you tear down the old set-up, you'd better check the idea for the improved method with your boss. You might also want to check it with the people whose work might be affected by the change, such as customers, subsequent users of the work, and even suppliers.

By simplifying your own job you will find that the time saved can be used to your advantage, and you'll get the same amount of work done with less effort; or, more importantly, you'll get more results with the same amount of effort.

Chapter 14
Organizing Other People's Work
To Make Them Help You More

Everyone knows how hard it is to remain within a budget, either at work or at home. To some it seems to be a foolish and unnecessary exercise, but ultimately a basic truth dawns upon all of us. There simply aren't enough resources to go around and unless we husband them carefully they will run out before we have been able to accomplish what we hoped for.

In Chapter Nine we outlined a three-step system for sharpening your effectiveness in action. The first stage was setting objectives. The next was controlling activities and eliminating those that didn't contribute to objectives. Finally, the third stage consists of converting your program into resources devoted to that program and of controlling those resources of time, dollars, space and people.

Keys to Creative Budgeting

The old method of budgeting was to treat the money as if it were being doled out of a bag. In fact, the French word for bag is bouget, which sounds a lot like budget. The implication is there is just so much money in the sack and when it is gone everything stops. This is true for some kinds of budgeting, but it isn't true for all kinds.

Accounting and budgeting merely measure the financial consequences of what is really happening. The control of resources, especially human resources, is what should concern us more than financial statements. Financial records are historical whereas human behavior is dynamic, creative and active. This is the area in which to start budgeting.

Let's go back and look at the systems approach to getting things done. We note that the inputs are used up in order to get the outputs. These inputs include three major categories of resources and are the best guide to controlling the resources.

- Labor is a major input. It can be measured in numbers of people, in man-hours (one person does one hour's work), man-days, man-months, or some similar measure.

- Materials and supplies are the physical things that go into what we are producing, or that are used up in producing and distributing it. **Direct materials** are the things that are used in producing the product itself; **indirect materials** are things which are used in producing the product itself; indirect materials are things which are used in producing the product or achieving the objective but, which don't appear in ther product itself. Thus, materials and supplies include such things as utilities, small tools, soap, lubricants, paper and so on.

- Capital is the investment which is required to get to the objective. We call it a **fixed investment** if it is something like a building, a machine, or land. It is called **working capital** if it is in the form of inventories, receivables owed to us by customers, or cash needed to operate the enterprise.

You'll get much farther in controlling resources in your system if you treat each of these three categories sepatately. In this book, however, we deal mainly with human resources.

Labor as as Input

We hear about "labor efficiency" in the popular press. This means that we are interested in the number of units produced (output) for the units of labor input. Keeping this ratio in mind is an important principle in controlling labor cost.

Staffing ratios are vital. The fact that a sales territory has two sales people doesn't mean that it is twice as costly as another if the two produce more than twice as much as the territory that has only one sales person. This is the concept of "unit cost." If you look at the simple example in Figure 14-1 you'll see that Department A is more **productive** than Department B, but Department B is more **efficient** than Department A. In terms of contribution to profit–the objective here–the chances are high that Department B is actually more profitable.

Production output	Department A 9100 units	Department B 7500 units
Foremen	2	1
Inspectors	1	1
Workers	91	65

Figure 14-1

Measure profit, not volume. Volume alone in sales, production or output doesn't mean greater efficiency. Take the case of the milk salesman illustrated in Figure 14-2. On the surface it looks like a mixed picture. This year the salesman did better on the latter two items but worse on fluid milk sales. On the other hand, since his objective is profit, we must judge upon a more realistic basis. What is the level of profit for each item? Suppose profit is 3 cents per quart on sales of fluid milk, 10 cents on a pound of cottage cheese. How would you then estimate which represented the best use of the salesman's time?

	Last Year	This Year
Fluid Milk Sales	3000 qts.	2600 qts.
Butter sales	450 lbs.	600 lbs.
Cottage cheese sales	300 lbs.	600 lbs.

Figure 14-2

Many sales people miss this point and spend all of their time, or most of it, on items where the margins of profit are smaller. As a result, they may actually produce less profit by bringing in a larger sales volume. The important point in these illustrations is not how sales people should spend their time, but how you can analyze your own efficiency in using your own labor.

Work at highest skill level. This is often a problem with bosses who insist upon doing their own subordinates' jobs for them. They are being paid a higher salary to perform higher level (more profitable) work. When bosses don't see the greatest opportunities for performing at their highest skill level they may be lowering their efficiency while at the same time working harder than ever.

Your effectiveness is diminished any time you work at a task that is using less skill than you have. Obviously, we can't all work at our highest level of capacity and skill at all times. You will do such things as drive your own car instead of hiring a chauffeur; you will fill out your own reports instead of hiring a clerk, when it would be uneconomic to do otherwise. The principle is still a good one. Using the services of others and paying a fair wage for them may be economical if it frees you for higher level work which is paid for at the higher rate.

> **The major barrier to using the full talents of people in an organization isn't economy, however, but often an outgrowth of some emotional attachment to the lower level of work. Willingness to concentrate on the important, higher level work is a sign of efficiency.**

The fair day's work. All of the above dicussion of the use of human resources deals with the "manning table" and the **utilization** of talents at the proper level. These are vital to getting maximum output from the labor input. Beyond this there is also the variable of a "fair day's work" which is important in maximum value form labor inputs, either your own or others.

Years ago, and even now in some of the more backward quarters, many boses assumed that laziness or slow-down was the only thing that could possibly account for the differences in productivity of people at work. Douglas McGregor called this "Theory X": that the average person dislikes work and will avoid it when he or she can and thus must be intimidated or controlled to turn out a fair day's work. McGregor pointed out a modern "Theory Y": that the average person finds work as natural and pleasant as rest or play and will produce if he or she has a goal and a reason for getting there.

Even if you assume that a person isn't lazy and that he or she wants to work, you might still improve the individual's productivity (or your own) by calculating what comprises a fair day's work, if only to provide a goal at which the worker or professional can shoot.

Others might also note that it gives you a yardstick for assessing whether or not you are getting as much return on the same investment in labor as the next person. It provides a system of measurement and prediction and can be the take-off point for improving effectiveness.

How do you determine what is a fair day's work? There are six steps in such a calculation if you are to do a complete job.

1. **Define the unit of work to be used.** Estimating a fair day's work begins with selecting a "unit" to be measured or studied. This is a task, product, job or output against which hours of manpower are to be matched. Remember that you are trying to find out what should be produced (output) in a labor hour, day or year (input). If, for example, a worker in a pin factory is part of an assembly line of ten workers who produce 100,000 pins per hour, the average output per man-hour would be stated as 10,000 pins, even if none of the ten workers produced a complete pin by himself or herself. Some examples of unit measurement for purposes of estimating work include:

dozens of eggs packed	hundredweight of flour bagged
gross of zippers sewn	number of sales calls made
patient days in hospital	number of welfare clients serviced

2. **Spell out the elements which make up the job unit.** This means that you turn to the work being done and break it down into small steps and list each step. Anything that advances the work is a step. Take the laborer who carries boxes to be worked upon to some machines. As you can see in Figure 14-3, it doesn't take a whole minute to complete the cycle, and, if you weren't careful or reasonable, you might assume that this would be the basic unit which when divided into the total minutes in the working day would comprise the "fair day's work." Actually, it would be unreasonable and not fair at all.

Name of the job: Materials Handler
Purpose: To transport boxes from aisle to machine
Output: One box every sixty seconds

Step	Operation	Time
1.	Observe the machine to note when another box is required	10 sec.
2.	Walk over and pick up a box	10 sec.
3.	Carry the box over to the machine	10 sec.
4.	Set the box down, return to observation position, and start the cycle over	10 sec.
	total actual cycle time	40 sec.

Figure 14-3

---

3. **Add in waiting, getting ready and putting away time.** This is the time lost in handling unforseen time-consumers, getting the boxes set

up before they are moved, and cleaning up the work area. Even though this is estimated, you still charge it against the basic cycle just as if it were part of the cycle. You might find, for example, that a fifth step world need to be added to the operation described in Figure 14-3. Thus you might allow ten seconds for waiting, making ready and putting away time. This increases the unit time to fifty seconds, but there is still going to be some lost time due to personal relief, coffee breaks and unexpected delays (such as machine breakdowns) that will occur from time to time. There may also be a slowing down due to worker fatigue late in the day. This adds a sixth step to the operation: ten seconds for personal time, fatigue and delay. You'll note that the cycle time for the six steps, of which two are estimated, is now one minute. This is the basic cycle time. You may now calculate what the average worker may be expected to produce over a full day. Even though the time for an individual cycle will in all likelihood come out closer to forty seconds, for purposes of planning how much labor input will be required you use the fair day's cycle.

4. **From a single cycle figure the full day's output.** In this case we have seen that the worker, day in and day out, should be able to produce (move) one box per minute, sixty per hour. This is realistic because it allows for regular recurring delays, fatigue and other factors. You now have the basis for your input-output calculations: One man-hour equals sixty boxes. If you know that fourteen hundred boxes must be moved each day, how many workers would you assign to this job? If they were all to be paid $3.50 per hour, what would be the cost of moving the boxes? You can quote this to your accountant who can price the product based upon such figures.

5. **Select and train workers.** With the elements of the job in hand and a knowledge of what comprises the best method and the expected output, you can now select and train workers. You choose people who can physically handle the work and whose qualifications are such that they won't quit after a day or so. You train them in the right way of doing the job, including any key points in the job which could make or break it, such as the safe way of lifting and proper way of handling boxes.

6. **Rate the efficiency of each worker.** As each person works, you are in an excellent position to rate the performance of his of her labor input. The "standard" time is sixty seconds per box, or four hundred eighty boxes per eight-hour day. If the person works at the job for only three hours, or six hours, your standard is still useful. You can rate how well you have used your manpower. The worker's efficiency is a ratio of how many boxes were actually moved to the standard amount which your estimate has shown should have been moved.

The idea here, of course, isn't to tell you how to rate a materials handler's job. You may be doing the same kind of estimating on any number of jobs, including your own. You might, for example, be estimating how many sales people it takes to cover a territory, how many maids to service a hotel, or how long it will take a typist to prepare invoices or shipping labels. The six steps will cover them all with a little practice on your part.

Let's add a word of caution here, however. You should go back and review the material on understanding human behavior in Chapter Seven now. It's vital to remember that people are not machines and that if they are treated as machines they'll slow down or quit. Being rational doesn't eliminate the need for being human. On the other hand, being fair and decent doesn't mean you aren't going to be rational, either.

PART IV
ACTIVATING OTHERS

If you've reached the conclusion from the last section that being personally effective in controlling situations is purely logical, you'll learn something from the following section. In it is suggested that the vital ingredient in taking action for success in the real world is moving people–persuading them, directioning them, consulting them, selling them. A formula is proposed that has been researched extensively by academic behavioral scientists. Expressed in plain language, it starts with "tell 'em," moves on to "sell 'em," and winds up with the best–"consult 'em."

We'll then turn to two kinds of situations in which you'll confront other people–the one, face-to-face with individuals; the other, small groups and conferences.

Chapter 15
Three Keys to Activating Other People to Go Your Way

If we want some result that calls for cooperation on the part of others, how do we go about moving them? There are three alternative paths we might follow:

1. **We can simply tell them to do it.** If we want to make this method work, we often let them know why with convincing reasons as, "If you don't, you're fired," or "Because the president wants it done." In some cases it may simply be, "Because I said so, dammit."

2. **We can sell them on doing it.** This is a well known process of pointing out the features of some new way of doing things, explaining benefits to the doers, showing people how others have benefited from doing it, and getting an agreement from people to try the new thing.

3. **We can point up the result desired and consult them.** Unlike the other two methods of activating people, here we ask others for their best ideas and we even ask whether the result is the best one to be sought. Having participated in the development of the idea, people become ego involved and go toward the goal as committed rather than coerced or persuaded.

Which one of these methods is best? This question has been the subject of an amazing amount of discussion, debate and research by behavioral scientists in recent years.

McGregor's Theory X and Theory Y

The late Douglas McGregor, eminent behavioral scientist from the Massachusetts Institute of Technology, spelled it out into two polar opposite alternatives.

- The hard-line or "tell 'em what to do" approach he called Theory X–a set of assumptions that the order giver carries around causing him or her to give orders rather that to ask people or to sell them. Theory X assumes that the average person dislikes work and avoids it whenever possible, and is lazy, uncooperative and perhaps a little dishonest.

- Theory Y, on the other hand, assumes that people like to work and find it as natural as rest or play, and that creativity is widespread in the population. Therefore, you can rely on people to be productive and creative when they know the goal and have a reason for wanting to get to it, such as when they see advantages to them in seeking the goal.

Debates in university classes and executive development courses as to which theory is true are, of course as foolish as the assumption that you must choose one or the other. The question is, under what circumstances should you assume that Theory X is true and when should you consider Theory Y as true, and under what conditions are neither of them perfectly true?

Autocratic Versus Democratic Styles

Numerous psychologists have used the same pattern of polarized thinking to divide activating styles into a continuum which resembles X versus Y. They use a three-part scale which, like Theory X and Theory Y, has two polar opposite conditions ("autocratic" and "laissez faire"), but it also has a middle ground ("democratic") in which the leader is responsive but doesn't give up all leadership functions. This is in contrast to the "laissez faire" style in which the leader doesn't give any orders but lets the group make up its own mind on anything it chooses. Laisez faire is a French term which, liberally translated, means "hands off." This means that the leader never directs things but keeps hands-off the decisions.

Like the debate over Theory X and Theory Y, the question is the same: Which one do you use in what situation? The idea that one or the other is a universal solution is, of course, a kind of idealistic or emotionally preconceived bit of nonsense. Of course.

Blake's Grid Theory

Much closer to reality is Professor Robert Blake's Grid Theory. It suggests that there is a style of management that can be described in a

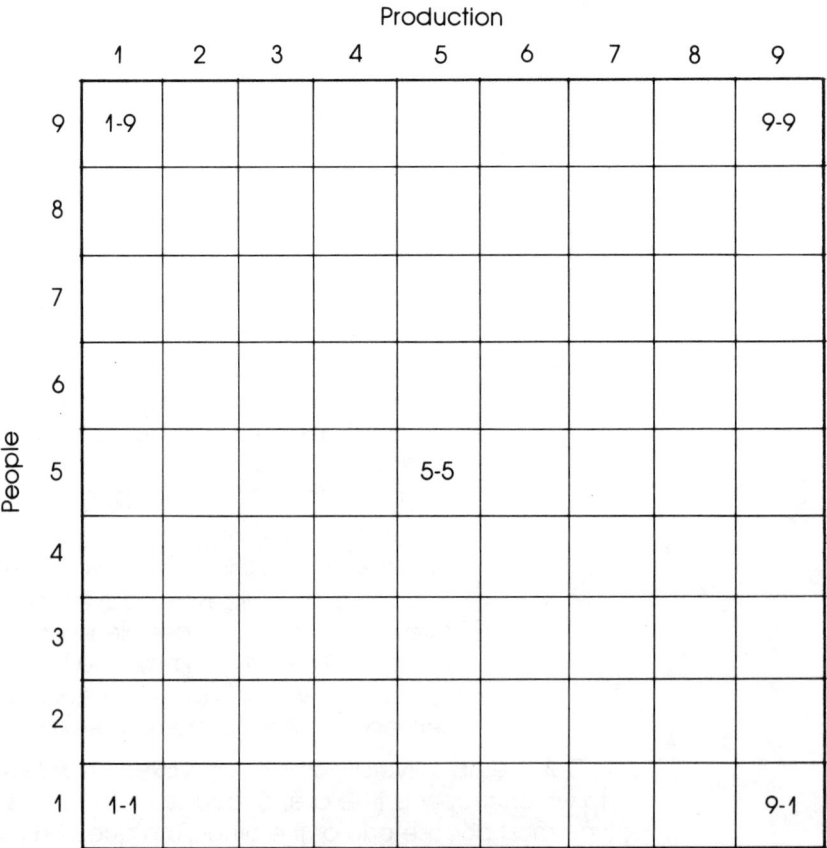

Figure 15-1

grid. The best outcome, he suggests, is position 9-9 in which you have combined the best features of all of the others while avoiding many of the unfortunate consequences of each.

As illustrated in Figure 15-1, the left vertical line of the grid represents the amount of concern for people. The horizontal scale represents concern for production and getting the job done. If you direct people at the 1-9 position with maximum concern for people and minimun concern for getting the job done, you are running a country club. On the other hand, if you are operating at the 9-1 position with maximum concern for production and minimum concern for people, you are running a sweat shop. Either position will have an adverse effect upon results, and a 5-5 position is a kind of cheap compromise that doesn't get the best effects of either. The optimal way is the 9-9 style. Here you emphasize getting maximum production while providing maximum satisfaction to the people doing the work.

This still leaves us with the question of whether you should ever vary from this idea, and how you average out at this fine level.

How to Choose an Appropriate Leadership Style

There are three important factors to watch in choosing which of the three leadership styles to select in moving others. These are:

First, **the leader himself or herself.** Some people are incapable of giving a tough order. Others find that selling isn't in their nature. And still others must relate to the world by overpowering it and couldn't listen to another person's opinion if their lives depended upon it. There are other personal characteristics that determine the style a leader should use as well, but this is one important variable.

Second, **the followers.** Managing engineers is different from managing foundry workers, for example.

Third, **the situational environment.** (This was spelled out in greater detail in earlier chapters.)

When to Give Direct Orders

Let's run through these three factors to see how things should look if you are to be an order giver.

Be autocratic when the leader:
- has complete power and resistance is practically impossible;
- is hampered by few practical restraints on the use of his or her power;
- has a way, in an emergency, that will save the whole crew (as, for example, the captain of a plane in trouble);
- has some unique knowledge that the rest of the people don't have;
- is firmly entrenched in his or her position and probably cannot be unseated.

Be autocratic when the followers:
- are dependent or helpless persons;
- have never had their opinions asked before and would be surprised, chagrined or frightened if they were asked of them now;

- are a temporary crew, a makeshift gang, or a one-time work force;
- know there is an emergency and are looking for help;
- are autocrats themselves who manage their own people autocratically and who expect that their leaders will be autocratic (and if they're not, they'll show signs of anxiety or scorn);
- are low on independence drives;

Be autocratic when the situation has these characteristics:
- There is an emergency and there's no time for explanations.
- All decisions have been made and discussion of the merits and demerits of the course of action selected would be useless.
- Time presssures are heavy and deadlines are close at hand.
- Physical dangers to people are involved unless they move quickly in unity.
- There's little judgment or decision making called for.
- A number of drastic changes must be made quickly.

If all of the above conditions exist, then the chances are pretty good that snappy order-giving will be the best leadership style. On the other hand, change the situation, the followers, and the leader—or any one of them—and you may be required to adopt a different style.

When to Sell Selling implies that the customer can refuse to buy, but it also implies that he or she can also be sold. The person may want to put up some sales resistance, discuss personal reservations about the proposed action, and get answers to questions before making a commitment.

Use salesmanship when the leader:
- has some authority, but not absolute power;
- could be unseated by the group if people really banded together, but this could not be done easily;
- is under some time pressures, but these pressures are not overly strong;
- has some sanction that can be exerted, but doesn't have ultimate power;
- is generally better informed than the group, but yet the group has some real expertise in some area which is superior to that of the leader;
- knows the objectives, but doesn't know all of the obstacles to reaching them that his or her followers may know.

Use salesmanship when the followers:
- expect some control over objectives from the top,

but want to have considerable say about how the job is to be done;
- like to work when things are systematized, but don't enjoy personal dictatorial authority over them;
- are in moderately short supply, but are willing to work in an organization and for a leader;
- frequently have middle class backgrounds and values;
- know their own interests and personal objectives and expect that these will be respected.

Use salesmanship when the situation meets these requirements:
- The general goals of the organization are understood and accepted by everyone concerned (as when it is known, for example, that the company is in business to make a profit, but it may not be clear just how your idea will contribute to that profit).
- The controls that exist are understood and have worked in the past, and people and used to them.
- Any changes in the organization usually come in regular but steady patterns;
- Dangers could be created if people went off on their own without unity and, knowing this, want to avoid disaster.
- Moderate to high skills are called for to achieve objectives.

When to Consult

There are certainly times when it is sound practice to consult the people you wish to activate. This involves the same three variables: the leader, the followers, and the situation. When should you practice consultative leadership?

Use consultative leadership when the leader:
- has no power to compel action even if he or she tries;
- is incapable of "tough" action;
- lacks a desire to dominate anyone;
- has nothing to withhold and has benefits to give;
- is dependent for tenure in his or her present office upon the pleasure of the group and can be fired by the group;
- has no special knowledge that the group lacks and is wholly dependent upon its good will, support and cooperation.

Use consultative leadership when the followers:
- have more power than the leader and know it;
- dislike orders and will react unfavorably if they receive them;
- can rebel if they choose to and will probably be successful;

- have firm ideas on what the goals and methods should be and will be diligent in assuring that they will be pursued;
- are volunteers, loosely organized, independently wealthy and/or have marketable job skills;
- are hard to recruit and could depart easily.

Be consultative when these characteristics exist in the situation:
- There are no clear purposes for the existence of the organization.
- The organization was formed solely to serve the pleasures or enrichment of the members, as is the case with a social club or recreation group.
- No agreement has been made that the leader should keep office beyond the time desired by the group.
- There are no time pressures whatsoever.
- The environment is safe, placid, or bland.
- The situation call for great individual contribution in the form of creativity or judgment.
- Changes have been few or have come gradually.

The Trend Is Toward Participative Management

In fact, you've probably concluded, there are few situations that would be clear-cut instances of one type of leadership to the exclusion of others. The number of variations of style will be as great as the the number of leaders, followers and situation which can exist in the real world. You'll probably find yourself using mixtures of all three leadership styles in every case.

The skill to be acquired is a kind of mature discrimination as to what the situation requires.

We might note that in both businesses and nonprofit organizations the trend is increasingly toward participation of the followers in the decisions that affect them.

Where is a safe beginning point for you? Generally, until you find out differently, it's wise to start at some middle ground of practice–around the "democratic" style (though Professor Gordon Lippit suggests that the prevailing style of leadership in industry today leans slighty toward the "autocratic" side of the three-point scale). Your own skill development, plus your own personal preference as to the kind of leader you'd like to be, will probably determine your method and its location on the scale.

It is also important to note that there is some predictability in your choice of style because of your self-fulfilling needs. If you believe that autocracy is the only style that will work with your followers, then you will shortly discover that they are behaving as if they need to be dictated to. On the other hand, if you believe that your followers will respond favorably to democratic or consultative leadership, you will surely discover that they do respond well to such treatment.

Chapter 16
Three Steps to Motivation

One of the great issues of leadership is that of motivation. No management conference is complete without speakers who have a current theory of motivation, a system of motivation, or some procedures for motivating employees.

Motivation is an explanation of the behavior of individuals and groups. It is perhaps one of the most difficult and perplexing subjects in the leadership of people. Why do people do what they do, and how do we get them to do what we what them to do?

Motivation As an Explanation of Behavior

We might substitute the phrase "a proposed explanation of behavior" every time we hear the word "motivation." This might clarify the issue for us. "Behavior" is explained by psychologists as a kind of human activity that can be seen or measured.

If we could explain human behavior and the influences (inner and outer) that can be used in explaining that behavior, then perhaps we could predict it. And if we could predict that behavior, then perhaps we could control it. This is a function of leadership. Understanding employee behavior is an essential factor in managing people.

A variety of disciplines offer insight into the explanation of human behavior. The disciplines of psychology, and anthropology can be beneficial to the manager. Now it's not necessary for the manager to be either a psychologist, sociologist or anthropologist. He or she needs only to be a talented amateur in these disciplines.

> **The manager's purpose in understanding motivation isn't to rehash scholastic disciplines, but to lead employees toward organizational goals.**

The manager requires knowledge of motivational principles in order to apply them to particular situations which confront his or her leadership. Simply knowing the information, however, is not sufficient. The manager must know how to use that information skillfully.

Learning Motivation Theory

Perhaps the single most important influence in learning about motivation is personal experience. Managers learn by working with other people. They are constantly observing the behavior of others, and a portion of this experience will be retained to become part of the manager's memory to be used in the future for problem and decision making.

Practical experimentation is another way of learning human behavior from personal experience and observation. This method of learning is common, but is perhaps the slowest and most costly in terms of wasted effort and energy. Occasionally it can even lead us to misinformation because our sample was either too small or rather special.

The second source of information concerning motivation is the experience of others. This is a function of education. It implies that a manager can be educated and can learn keen insights through the study of human relations in the literature. The behavioral sciences are one good source of this kind of information. But much can be gained through insights into the minds of workers, managers and other people in the organization. We can learn as much about human relations by reading such authors as Ralph Waldo Emerson and James Boswell as we can Chris Argyris, Rensis Likert and Frederick Herzberg.

Closely allied to reading the works of authors on human behavior is studying the observations of others on behavior and discussing the topic with them. This includes executive development conferences and the "learn by learning" concept. This is the exchanging of experiences. This approach provides a sense of practicality that is not apparent in studying the literature of the behavioral sciences.

A third way of learning about human behavior involves scientific observation, experiment and statistical analysis. We rely here upon scientific observations and trained professional experimenters to conduct the behavioral scientists. Their purpose is not the establishment of value systems that remain outside the realm of science, but the discovery of "truth" as it is.

The manager, then, acquires insights, knowledge and information from these three sources which can be applied to predict and control the behavior of his or her subordinates.

Influences on Behavior

A complete theory of motivation would encompass many areas for understanding. Our knowledge of human behavior should take into account these seven factors:

1. We should understand that people have a biological mechanism that causes them to behave in certain ways. If a person has a biological problem, his or her behavior may become inadequate.

2. We should look at the backgrounds of people with a view toward using this information in changing human behavior. A person's upbringing and environment have a definite and profound impact upon curent behavior patterns.

3. We should become familiar with the range of human motivations, how activtiy is generated, and what happens when the activity is frustrated.

4. We should look at the person's emotional structure and the range of emotions which govern his or her behavior (rage, love, fear, happiness, and so on). These furnish knowledge to identify where the person is now, and perhaps to predict where he or she might be in the future.

5. We should look at the nature of learning and apply the principles to the study of human behavior.

6. We should look at communications abilities and the underlying principles with regard to human beings.

7. We should learn something about the mentally disturbed. The number of emotionally disturbed persons is increasing, and it is likely that most managers will confront disturbed individuals. A knowledge of the range of disturbances would be useful in dealing with such individuals.

A Three-Factor Theory of Motivation

What can a manager do to cope with the motivational problems that face him or her? I suggest an affirmative approach to motivation—a three-factor theory of motivation. The three factors are:
- the effective use of information;
- the effective removal of obstacles;
- the skillful use of payoffs.

We'll look at each of these factors in turn.

The Objective As a Motivator

The Effective Use of Information. The first step in motivating people is to tell them exactly what is expected of them. We should not concern ourselves with inner drives, personality factors, or inner arrangements, but with the direction we wish people to move toward the ultimate goal we have in mind. The objective is the first motivational force. The point is to stress external information within the control of the boss to present information regarding what is expected.

A study done for the American Management Associations showed that the most common kind of missing information in superior/subordinate communication is that related to job objectives. Left to their own devices, the manager and subordinate will fail to agree on what is expected.

To put this first factor to work, each manager and subordinate sit down and talk each quarter about what is expected in terms of job performance. This is then confirmed by a written memo with a copy for the superior and on for the subordinate. This memo clarifies the conditions that will exist if the job is either well done or poorly done. It tells the person which direction to go in. It tells what this means in terms of success or failure. It defines a range of possible outcomes, successes and failures, and it offers simple information about the job.

The motivational effects of the three categories of objectives (regular, problem solving and innovative) are described in Figure 16-1.

Supportive Management As a Motivator

The Effective Removal of Obstacles. The second factor in the three-factor theory of motivation is a function of the boss which entails obstacle removal. It means supportive management on the part of the higher level executive.

> The supportive manager is one who asks: "Is there anything I could do, do differently, or stop doing that would help my subordinates reach the objectives we have agreed upon?"

A leader has certain responsibilities to forsee the unfavorable consequences that stand in the way of success. Sometimes the obstacles lie in physical facilities. The obstacle removing activities of the boss include the removal of barriers to information.

The second factor in the three-factor theory of motivation is making sure that the job can be done; making sure that the way is cleared.

B. F. Skinner, the noted behavioral scientist, believes that obstacle removal is perhaps the most complete explanation of changed behavior. The social contingencies, as he describes them, are extremely important to human behavior. If we can arrange the environment to stimulate favorable behavior, people will behave favorably.

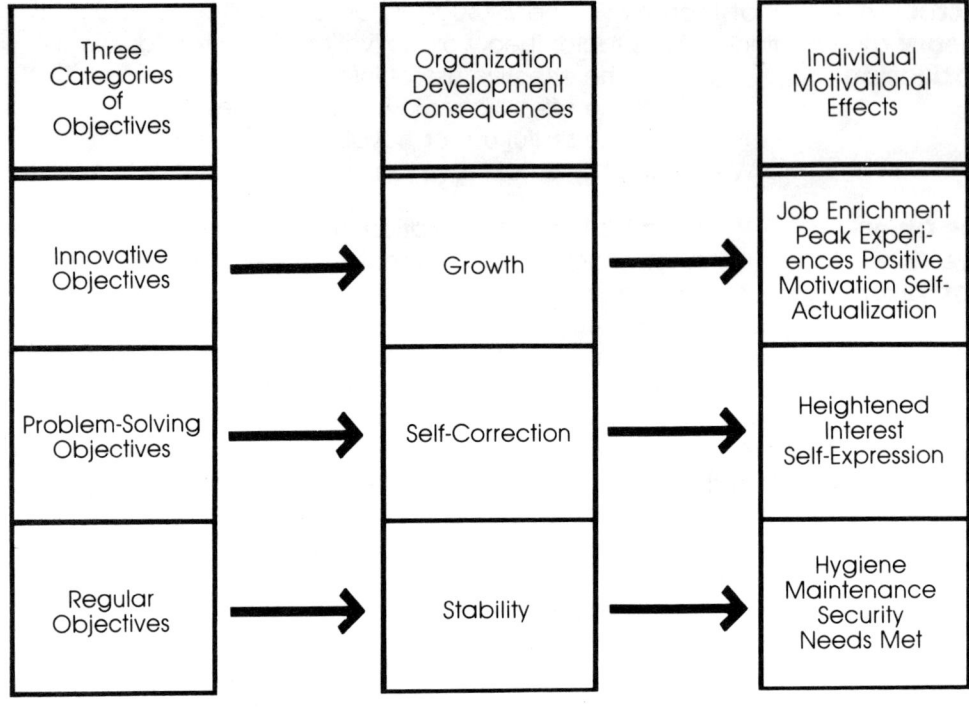

Figure 16-1

Rewards As Motivators

The Skillful Use of Payoffs. We are all familar with the third factor because it has to do with rewards. Classical economists suggested that people were economic beings and that as such they worked for money and for money alone. This assumption underlies many of our management systems today. But while it is evident that people need money, behavioral scientists have taught us that money is not the only motivator. It is perhaps not even the most important motivator.

Understanding motivation from the behavioralist's point of view begins with the physical needs. Once these are met, however, they no longer comprise a motivator. The individual then seeks out new forms of motivation, looking for new forms of input to satisfy himself or herself. These satisfactions are nonmonetary in nature.

Perhaps people need the satisfaction of being respected by their peers. Or maybe they need the recognition of knowing what is expected of them and knowing how well they are doing. Or they want a sense of belonging. They may want to feel adequate. They may want to feel that they are good at something. And they may be looking for a way to express their creativity.

Abraham Maslow has arranged these human needs into a hierarchy explaining that if a person lacks something in the physical sense, this physical need will become preeminent over all others. But once all physical needs are filled, ego satisfaction is sought. From this point we move on to self-actualization—the highest level of needs. This is realizing the very best a person can be.

Motivators and Demotivators

Frederick Herzberg has classified various factors, stating that there are certain kinds of factors that aren't really motivators at all. They are simply demotivators if they aren't present.

The absence of certain aspects of compensation or working conditions may just slow a person down. These demotivators he calls "hygiene factors." This doesn't mean that if a person gets good fringe benefits or high pay or good facilities that he or she will be motivated. It merely means that if these things are not present, the person is not motivated.

The true motivators, according to Herzberg, lie in the work itself. They lie in those aspects of the work that permit the person to grow, to develop, to excel. These are similar to Maslow's "peak experiences." If people can find such peak experiences in their work, these will be their most creative and productive moments. The nature of peak experiences varies from individual to individual.

Chapter 17
Face-To-Face Communication Makes Things Happen

Academic researchers who have investigated the use of time in business have found that people in technical, managerial, professional or sales postitions spend almost seventy-five per cent of their time meeting and talking with other people.

These are activities which involve the individual and which can be improved upon and developed with practive and coaching. Much of personal effectiveness in the symbol manipulating world in which we live is word skills. The kinds of conversations in which we engage can easily be classified into the three categories discussed in the previous chapter–you may converse with people to tell 'em, to sell 'em, or to consult 'em.

Conversations that Instruct

The principal use of the one-way conversation is in that kind of instructional conference in which an informed speaker is transmitting knowledge to an uninformed listener. This presupposes several conditions:

First, the teacher is transmitting a kind of factual knowledge which doesn't require any attitude change. For example, if a physicist is going to explain atomic energy to a group of laymen, he would hardly want to conduct a democratic discussion. He knows the principles and the listeners don't. We should avoid faking democratic discussions when transmission of new knowledge to an unlearned person is the objective. Just go ahead and tell 'em.

Second, the person receiving the information is intelligent enough to be able to understand the information. This may also imply that he or she knows the jargon which will be used. Nothing is more irritating than listening to somebody explain something in vocabulary which is totally foreign. A statement such as "The cut-edge overlap of the side seam should be within a plus or minus tolerance of two-tenths" would have great value to the experienced person who has worked in a particular shop for years and might even be helpful new knowledge, but to the completely new person it would only be confusing.

A variation of this is a habit which many people persist in pursuing. They use inside jokes, local terms, or first names of people whom the listener couldn't possibly know, just as if they were fully aware of every term, every name, and every past event with which the speaker is familiar. Take the conversation I heard recently between a young GI and a motherly lady in an airport: "I'm lucky to be here," the GI said. "The CQ was supposed to have my TD orders cut, but they'd been sent to Regimental CP with the morning report." The lady looked neutral and said, "That's nice." What else could she say?

The principle of show-and-tell is helpful when you are presenting new information for the first time. The old World War II method of Job Instruction Training is still the best method of presenting job information to new people. JIT was an orderly process of teaching people who had never worked in an industry how to perform factory jobs for turning out defense products. More than thirteen million workers were trained by

this system. It has several specific steps:
1. Preparation
   - Break down the job to be taught into definite steps.
   - List all of the key points which will be important.
   - Get all of the tools, equipment and locations ready before instructing the worker.
   - Prepare the worker to get him or her ready to learn. Tell workers the purpose of the job, its importance and the reasons for doing it your way. Stress benefits, such as promotions or bonuses if they exist. Find out how much the worker already knows about this kind of work.
2. Presentation
   - Patiently show and tell the worker the job one step at a time.
   - Demonstrate each step as you describe it, and permit workers to ask questions. Constantly ask them to repeat your instructions. Stress the key points and make trainees repeat them.
3. Performance try-out
   - Immediately following the instructions, have the worker do the job and explain each step as he or she does it.
   - Correct every error as it occurs and have the trainee go back over it until you know that he or she is doing the job the right way.
   - Have the trainee teach the job to you as he or she is demonstrating.
   - Put the person on his or her own.
4. Follow-up
   - From time to time audit the worker's actual performance to see if he or she is using the proper method.
   - Arrange a way for the worker to get his or her questions asked and answered.

A key element of the JIT method is the responsibility for communicating lies with the teacher. If the learner hasn't learned, the teacher hasn't taught.

I would suggest that at this stage you take some time out from reading and try applying the JIT method descibed above to teach some simple operation familiar to you to some person near you who will cooperate–some member of your family, an employee, your secretary, or a colleague. Go back over the four-step plan and apply it to some simple job, such as one of these:
- Opening a fresh pack of cigarettes and lighting one.
- Tying a windsor knot in a necktie.
- Braiding a little girls' hair.
- Changing the cartridge in a ball point pen.

It may not be as simple as it appears. If it seems costly in time to teach people to do things right the first time, match this against the time consumed by doing the job over, patching up errors, or filling out accident reports when the job is improperly done.

Practice this four-step JIT plan when you are in instructional situations with individuals. The payback is immense.

Conversations That Sell Others

There are numerous formulae for selling. "AIDS" is one example. That's shorthand for Attention, Interest, Desire, Sale. More valuable, however, is the rule proposed by Arthur Deegan, a successful sales and marketing man whose courses in personal persuasion have been of invaluable assistance to others. Deegan emphasizes that selling conversations involve a person-to-person relationship.

This approach is based on four basic needs which have been found by psychologists to be common to all of us.

1. **Recognition.** We all desire to be told that we are important, even if it is only temporarily. Customers feel that they should be treated as important people and they want the kind of recognition that indicates that they are respected and their business is valued. This doesn't require grovelling or subservience, but respectful and sincere interest and attention.

2. **Belonging.** Everyone desires to feel that he or she "fits in." When meeting a salesperson for the first time we want to know that the relationship is normal and that our performance as a customer is OK. Growls, indifference or mere tolerance destroys this relationship.

3. **Adequacy.** Many people live in fear of being wrong or being found inadequate. The high-hat sales person who makes the customer feel out of place gives the customer feelings of inadequacy. By eliminating any embarrassment and making customers feel comfortable, the sales person can quickly dispel the customer's feelings of ignorance and helplessness.

4. **Security.** We all desire to be able to predict with any reasonable certainty what will happen to us and what our relationships will be. In selling to people, the salesperson should put customers at ease so that they feel confident and relaxed in their relationship with the seller.

The key to successful selling and to repeat sales is the establishment of a personal relationship between the seller and the customer. This is what makes a regular customer out of a browser or a one-tme buyer. The trick is to make each customer feel welcome and to give him or her the red carpet treatment. The technique for putting a welcome mat in front of your customer is very simple–just act the way you do when a friend calls at your home.

Conversations That Motivate

The third category of face-to-face conversations is that which involves treating another person consultatively. The main idea here is to help other people help themselves. You hope to discover insights with other people that will cause them to change their own behavior. Here's a three-step plan for conversations that motivate people through consultation:

- Become inolved with the other person;
- Use nondirective listening methods;
- Summarize the conversation and action agreed upon.

Let's look at each step in a little more detail.

Become Involved with the Other Person. The first step in consultative conversations that motivate people is to make the person feel important by showing sincere and friendly interest in the indvidual and in his or her problems.

- Make the other person the central figure. Treat his or her opinions as more important than your own. Find out his or her objectives and the obstacles to reaching them. Learn how the other person feels about the situation.
- Recognize your own prejudices, if you have any, know what effect they could have and are having upon effective listening in face-to-face conversations. You can't get rid of all of your likes and dislikes, but keep them under control.
- Listen in order to understand. You have one purpose in a consultative face-to-face conversation: to understand the other person's position. You might not agree with it, but at least you'll understand it from the other person's viewpoint at the end of the conversation. Find out what the other person's priorities are.

Use Nondirective Listening Methods. The second step is learning the technique of active listening, which isn't natural for most of us. In normal conversation we usually listen only long enough to wait for a break so we can jump in with our own views. This is a barrier to good listening. Nondirective listening is active, attentive listening to what the other person is saying.

- Try to keep the other person talking by keeping your own trap shut. Nod attentively to show you undrstand, and perhaps make noises of understanding such as, "I see" and "Uh-huh." If the person pauses, prompt him or her to tell you more.
- Encourage expressions of feelings. Don't fight back when the other person expresses emotional concerns. Simply accept them and don't argue or rebut or you'll bottle up the most useful kind of information that might be divulged.
- Repeat or phrase in different words what the other person says. Try to state the other person's position as you have heard it in exactly the same words. "I see, you felt let down because you didn't get the city territory."
- Don't use cross examination methods of questioning. Avoid leading or loaded questions such as,

"Wouldn't you be better off. . .?" or "Have you considered doing. . .?" Don't ask questions that can be answered "yes" or "no," but only those that will start the conversational flow of words from the other person.
- Listen for insights. When the conversation is flowing smoothly and the other person is spilling forth his or her ideas, goals, emotions and problems, somewhere in the midst of the stream will come some words of insight. "Now I see my problem as being. . ." At this stage you might move toward the third phase of consultative conversations. You are now ready for the action payoff. Be patient in waiting for insight to come and permit the other person ample time to keep talking. Once insight has come, don't let it get away.

Summarize the Agreements. In your rephrasing of the other person's comments, keep coming back to the insights you've found. Emphasize that it was he or she who stated the conclusion (not you), and that it was the other person who developed his or her own solution. "To summarize, what you have told me is that you feel that perhaps your failure to get the city territory was due to mediocre performance in your present job." The speaker may then go back to previous tirades, but keep rephrasing the insights until the other person accepts his or her own conclusions. Then state the problem for him and suggest he be ready when the territory opens up again in the future.

The whole idea is to help the person see his or her own problem and develop his or her own solution. This identification of problems and their solutions won't emerge in crystal clear form. They are apt to be mixed in with lots of irrelevant, emotional statements. You must listen to it all; and, by becoming involved and by mastering nondirective listening, you'll be able to get genuine commitment.

Simply pointing out the problem in the first place will do nothing but antagonize the other person and increase the emotional fervor. When a person is emotionally charged up, nondirective converstions are the only way out for you.

Remember that every time you talk with somebody you are bringing certain things with you into that conversation other than facts, procedures, suggestions and policies. You are bringing a set of problems, experiences, interests, objectives, feelings, abilities and viewpoints.

If you want to end a conversation fast, Professor Earl Brooks of Cornell University has catalogued a list of phrases he calls "boomerang phrases." Here are a few ill-chosen words which will wreck any converstion. We might call them "famous last words":

"If I were you, I would. . . " or "When I was. . . "
This is the use of the "big I." Actually, you're making the decision for the other person, whereas what you want to do is have the other person make his or her own decisions whereby action for improvement is

likely to be taken.

"What you say just isn't so. . . "

This one has proven to be a complete and long-remembered barrier to successful conversation.

"This is what you are going to do. . . "

This is another effective communication stopper. If you must use it, be sure you mean it and can back it up.

"If you would do. . . " or, even worse, "If you would do what Jim does. . . "

Compare people with standards, not other people.

"Fine, but. . . " or "Yes, but. . . "

This is the technique of a fast pat on the back followed by a knife in the same place.

"I told you so. . . "

You know the under-the-breath response to this one, too.

Chapter 18
Using Transactional Analysis
To Make Your Transactions Pay Off

Lots of people you know are games players. They not only play games like golf and tennis, but play games in thier transactions between people at work, between parents and children, and between husbands and wives. Your relationships with your competitors or colleagues on the job are a sort of game. There are three ways in which understanding how people play games can help you with your face-to-face relations, and make you more effective:

- You might be able to **avoid losing** if you understand how game playing is done.
- You might even understand **how to win.**
- Best of all, you might be able to understand **how to win yourself without causing someone else to lose.** That is, both of you are winners in a "win-win" combination.

The worst possible of all combinations is where you get engaged in some kind of a spitting match with somebody and you both lose. There are some people who want somebody else to lose so much that they are willing to lose themselves. These are the pathological cases who would blow themselves away with dynamite in order to blow up their enemy.

My presumption here is that you aren't pathological, but rather that you might be able to play the games better so that you produce more "win-win" combinations in your dealings with people.

Transactional Analysis

This kind of analysis is called Transactional Analysis or T.A. In other words, it seeks to analyze yours transactions–and show you how to analyze new ones while they are coming at you–so that you can turn "lose-win" situations into "win-win" transactions. The father of this kind of analysis is the late Eric Berne whose book **Games People Play** started a whole new kind of self-help training for effectiveness. You might want to get your own copy and read it.

Berne pointed out that when people get into transactions they become games players, and then proceeded to identify two major classes of games that people play:

1. **Pastimes.** These are important to our happiness, but are not life-affecting. We talk to others about the weather, athletics, our new cars or our old ones, and what our kids are doing or have done. All of this is necessary just to maintain the ordinary social relations we need. Berne calls this behavior between people "stroking." It's like scratching a cat behind the ears, patting a dog, or feeding a sugar cube to a horse. We don't really mean anything vital in doing so, but everybody plays the game. A pastime transaction is mainly significant if it is missing. We like that little social lubricant that makes our day go by to indicate that we are in touch with the human race and that lets us know that we are recognized.

2. **Life games.** This second basic type of game is a lot more important. In face-to-face relations we ask people for a loan, we try to sell somebody a new product, we ask somebody to marry us, or we turn somebody down. We tell the teacher that Johny really should get into the math class, or we persuade the judge not to throw us in the slammer. Our credibility, our persuading ability and our major transactions are probably life games.

These face-to-face transactions cannot be understood, says Berne, unless you understand sonething about "ego states"–our inner personalities. To understand these, stick with this definition a bit further.

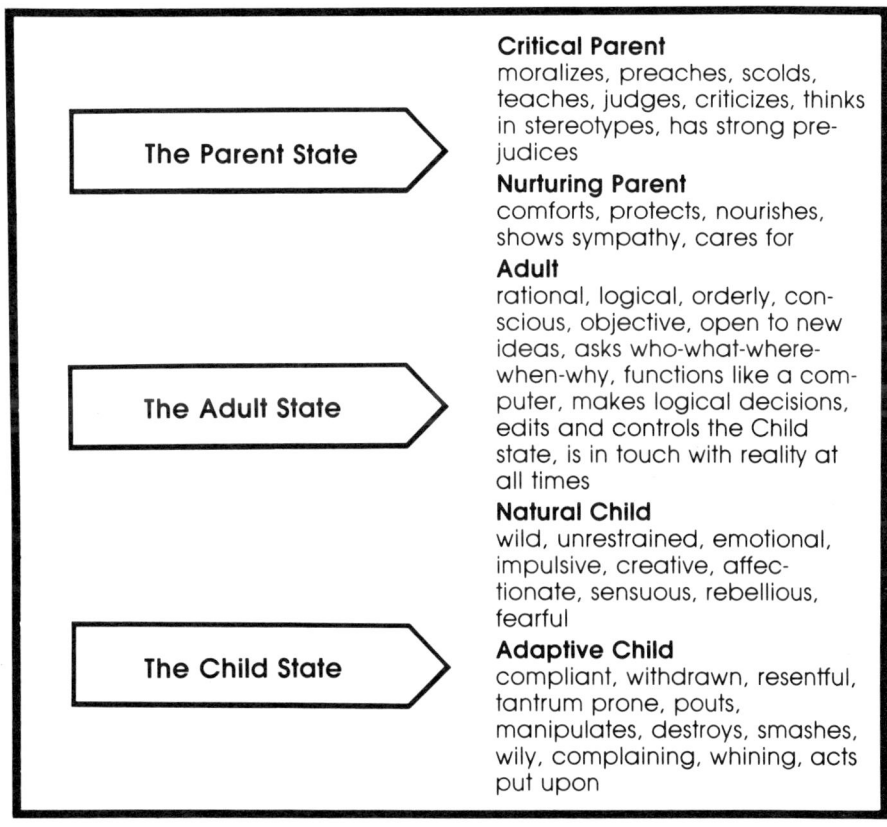

Figure 18-1

Berne found that people really aren't all of one mind (he calls it ego state) at any particular time. Rather, they have at least three ego states. When people are in one ego state they behave one way; when in another they behave differently. For example, he found that there are three major ego states (Figure 18-1) which we grow through as we grow up. Picture this as three different emotional (not physical) switching stations.

Since all people have these states, when two people get into a transaction, a series of several possible combinations can occur during the transaction. We are always switching from one state to another for some reason, usually because of some kind of game we are playing.

The important point is to know what ego state you are in at all times, and also what ego state the other peson is in.

What you really want is a "complementary" transaction, such as Adult-Adult. However, if you are dealing with a Natural Child, you may find that a Nuturing Parent state is best. The goal is effective transactions.

One of the effects of game playing is that people sometimes "cross" transactions in order to win the game (Figure 18-2). That is, one person starts out with an Adult request, but the other person tries to play the Parent. If this game succeeds, the first person will slip into a Child state and lose.

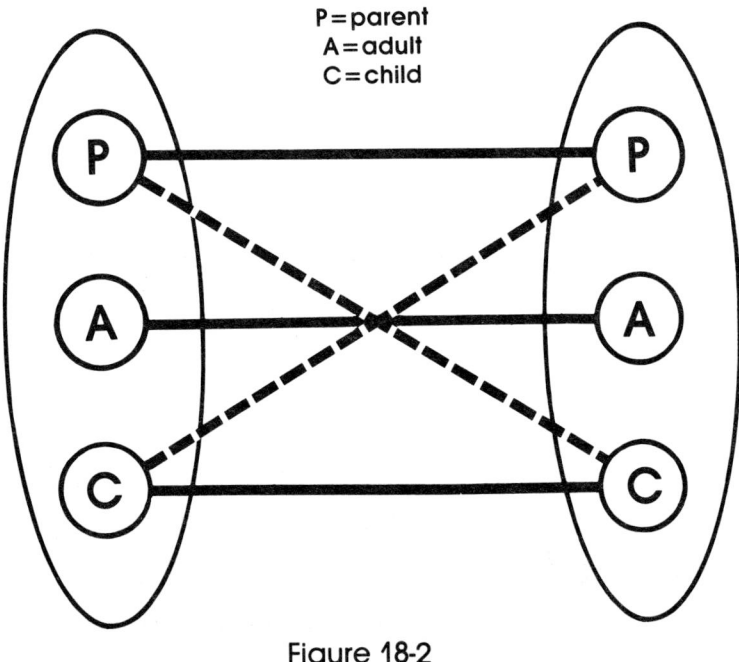

Figure 18-2

You can usually recognize what state a person is in (including yourself) by listening to the words being employed and by studying the expressions and behavior of people while they are speaking. The chart in Figure 18-3 will help you recognize some typical expressions for each of your ego states and those of the other person in face-to-face discussions. Using these and similar expressions, try listening to your own conversations for a few days and see if you can recognize your own states and those of the people with whom you are talking.

Knowing the three ego states and reognizing them while you are in transactions will help you keep your face-to-face relations on an Adult-Adult level, which is where most successful and effective behavior should tend most of the time.

Parent
"You see, when I was your age..."
"If you would only show some judgment."
"The trouble with you is. . ."

Adult
Listen (rephrase):
"I see, tell me more."
"What I hear you saying is. . ."
"Let me rephrase your statement."
"In other words you're saying that. . ."
Simple Acceptance:
"You 'messed up' as you put it."
"You often feel over your head."
"I understand how that must have embarrassed you."
"It is often painful to be dressed down by a customer."
"You'd rather be somewhere else than working tonight. It often is inconvenient to work evenings."
Insight:
"You think your problem is. . ."
"Where are you now?"
"Then the major crunch is. . ."
"In other words you don't control purchasing."

Child
"Why is everybody always picking on me?"
"Oh, heck, there's nothing I can do right anyway."
"I guess I'm a bum manager."

Figure 18-3

How TA Can Improve Your Effectiveness

If you've studied these suggestions closely you've noted that the emphasis has been upon getting you into a mode where your game playing should produce a "win-win" game for both sides. This takes more Adult-Adult transacting than any other combination. Here are some further hints you can try out in making TA work to improve your effectiveness and help you get where you want to go.

1. **Stick with the Adult state even when the other person doesn't.**

When confronted by hostile or domineering people, they are often trying to get you to revert to a Child state where you can be dominated by them. This situation requires that you find an Adult set of behavior and persist in it even when it is tempting to lash back. The car salesman (a classic type of intimidator) wants to put the transaction in a Parent-Child mode, with you as the Child. All provocations are attempts to get you to become Child-like. Avoid them.

2. **You can still retain an Adult ego state when you are angry.** It is possible to be angry as an Adult without becoming Child-like. Here are some examples:

Do This	Not This
"When you break your word I become angry because I waste time and money."	"You rotten liar. Why are you always such a sneaky fibber?"
"In my opinion your product isn't as good as that of other suppliers based on my studies."	"You make junk, and I think you are a sneaky crook."
"Frankly, I haven't made up my mind and will have to think it over and let you know later."	"I don't know what I want, or even what I think."

3. **The objective of TA is to play a "win-win" game; anything else is dangerous.** If you try to win by making the other person lose you risk later revenge, and perhaps losing yourself. You might also end up in a game in which both sides lose.

4. **Being Adult most of the time will help you overcome some tough face-to face situations.** If you can recognize, practice and finally master the Adult ego state in yourself despite pressures of the situation to force you into a into a Parental or Child state, you will be better equipped to deal with the following situations:
- When people withhold information: You can build trust and confidence by active listening and by showing understanding.
- When people manipulate information: You can make it clear that you are aware of the manipulation without being deceived or angered by rephrasing the information and asking for clarification.
- When people avoid critical issues: You can often use active listening, rephrasing and simple acceptance to draw people out to go on to arrive at insights when they paint a fake picture of themselves or the situation.
- When people attempt to put you down: You can restate what has been said when someone makes an unwarranted attack on you or others. Don't argue, but use simple acceptance to get them to expand until they have some insight.
- When people deprecate themselves and put themselves down: you can use rephrasing and simple acceptance to get them to expand until they get insights. Once insight is in hand you can help them turn to action to correct their views. ("Maybe you haven't succeeded, as you have put it. Is there anything we might do to make you more successful in the future?")

- When a person keeps changing the subject: People often try to evade the unpleasant by shifting from person to person and topic to topic, by making wisecracks, and by turning the conversation to something trivial. When this happens you can rephrase the words the person has used on the original subject back to the individual, constantly inviting him or her to return to the original subject. ("Let's go back to what you said first. I think you said you are perfectly happy with your work. Why do you think that way?")
- When people avoid the facts: Push for facts when people gloss over, generalize and glamorize the case without giving any real hard evidence for their conclusions. ("I understand that you are generally satisfied with the results, but can you give any specific examples that would justify the way you feel?")
- When people avoid feelings: People often wish to avoid stating their true feellings and wish to stay away from them. You can ease this situation by taking an Adult approach, watching and observing very closely not only what the person says but his or her apparent emotional condition while speaking. ("I see, you don't wish to be a member of the committee and I note that you apparently feel very strongly about this.")

Once you have mastered the Adult state you will discover that you are a much better listener and this will produce considerable improvement in your face-to-face effectiveness. People who are good listeners are often surprised when people subsequently describe them as "brilliant conversationalists." You will get more information, generate more support for your own ideas, and develop mutual trust by sound, active listening. This requires concentration upon the other person as well as skills in rephrasing and insights in your conversations.

Chapter 19
Working Effectively Through Small Groups

An important group of conferences was held in the Social Relations Department at Harvard University in the Fifties. Unlike some momentous conferences of heads of state, these were meetings of variously composed small groups of students. Every word and action was observed by trained social scientists who were studying what actually occurs in conferences. A number of important findings came out of this research and were originally published in a book written for other social scientists, but they have since been woven into management training courses for conference leaders and conference members. In this chapter we will deal with some practical aspects of being a conference member and a conference leader, and of communicating with small groups.

Understanding the Nature of Groups

The research on small groups is extensive and would require more space than is available here even to outline the major principles. Suffice it to say that the group has characteristics and behavior that can be studied, predicted and managed. The group, like the individual, develops purposes and norms of behavior for its members, and can use these norms to move the individual members forward energetically, or can subvert them into position movements of considerable influence and power.

Cliques, or informal organizations, often grow up inside formal organizations and can affect the behavior of individual members as much as the policies, pay systems and regulations of the formal organization.

In addition to this, the behavior of members of the group is reasonably predictable. There are roles that appear in many—or even most—groups which, if recognized, can make small group communications more effective. One such role is that of "convenor," the person who calls the meeting and opens it, suggesting the purpose and agenda. Often this individual serves as chairperson throughout the meeting, but isn't the only ingredient in the group's performance. Another role is that of the "idea man" who puts forth a veritable barrage of new and acceptable ideas that advance the meeting. Another role, played by a member, may be that of "best liked person" whose ability to ease the tension or to solve a puzzling block in the conference makes him or her liked by the other members of the group. Finally, there is a "blocker" whose opposition to what the rest of the group apparently wants slows down the progress and sometimes blocks the success of a small group meeting.

Small groups are usually considered to be "primary groups" in which the number of people in the session is small enough that all of the people can see and talk with one another. Usually this comes to no more than a dozen. One research study indicates that the most effective group size is five members. When it gets beyond that the simple mechanics of getting everyone to take part are hampered. When it drops to four the chance of a two-two split is present; and, when there are three, the term "consensus" can have no meaning, and the individuals simply don't jell as a group.

Conferences as Typical Small Groups

The most familiar of the business and voluntary association small group meetings is the conference or committee. Based upon the research and the experience of many such groups, we can not identify what makes for effective membership and leadership in a conference.

The three major purposes of conferences are (1) to solve problems, (2) to define policy, and (3) to train the participants.

The three requirements of a good conference are (1) that it starts with a reason for being called, (2) it includes people who can make a contribution, and (3) it is conducted systematically to move it toward a result.

The most common conference is one which is designed to solve a problem or several problems. The idea is to achieve several kinds of objectives. You want to achieve not only a solution of high quality in terms of logic but also to find one which will work because it is acceptable to the group members. When well conducted, a conference can be especially valuable in terms of this latter aspect–gaining acceptance of the solution. It is a form of participative leadership and permits all those available with informed opinion to discuss their own interests and to incorporate these countrary views into a solution through which group unity can be achieved.

- A conference provides for a pooling of experiences not readily obtainable through individual interviews.
- A conference draws on the power of suggestibility. The idea of Member A elicits a new idea suggested to Member B when he/she hears A.
- A conference blunts the criticism of the absent member who "wasn't consulted."

The leader plays a special active role, but doesn't dominate or manipulate the session. The leader's main job is to serve in the capacity of a switchboard operator in a live session giving everyone who has an opinion an opportunity to present it. The leader stimulates the dull members of the group who might not say anything and shuts off adroitly the monopolist who would dominate the whole meeting.

Like any skilled craftsman, the leader has certain tools for his or her use. They include the following:

1. **An agenda:** A list of things that should happen at the meeting and the order in which they should occur. The agenda is prepared in advance and is distributed so that the conferees will have a chance to prepare themselves before they arrive. If there is any detailed reading to be discussed, copies of it are sent out far enough in advance that meeting time needn't be consumed in reading it. If there are any questions to be resolved, they are stated in the agenda.

2. **Visual aids:** If something to be discussed can be visualized by making a chart, preparing a handout, or using a blackboard, these items are on hand when the meeting starts. During the meeting the leader uses such devices as the blackboard or chart pad to note in written form what the discussion has concluded; and common areas of agreement can be displayed for all to see.

3. **Questions, not lectures:** It's important to remember that a conference is not a "tell 'em" kind of session. The problem-solving conference is designed to get acceptance as well as to solve the problem, and sermons won't do the job. This doesn't imply that the conference leader is mute; the leader uses the basic tool of asking questions to steal the topic from the monopolist (by turning to ask someone else for his or her opinion, for example), to clarify points, and to stir up differences of opinion. Bland questions are used to stimulate further expression. Questions are used to summarize and to get commitments to action.

4. **Behavioral skills:** Through practice, the leader works hard at sharpening certain kinds of skills:
- thinking quickly and responding quickly;
- sufficient vocabulary and effective expression;
- thinking systematically by starting at the beginning, proceeding to the middle and going to the end;
- controlling his or her temper and emotions;
- learning to wait out the slow movers;
- resisting the temptation to "bop" people;
- maintaining a ready store of quips and cheery soothers.

No one, apparently, is born with these behavioral skills, and learning them takes time and practice. They aren't learned in isolation but in the give and take of conferences. The learning comes from trying them and getting feedback of successes and failures.

5. **Procedures:** There are a number of procedures or rules of the road which should be followed if a conference is to be effective. These include:
- advance notification of conferees and distribution of the agenda;
- a telephone reminder to the office of the late arriver, then convening of the meeting without the individual who wil show up on time at the next meeting (this avoids penalizing those who are prompt);
- a visual disply of the meeting's objectives on a blackboard or a chart pad throughout the meeting;
- introduction of conferees to each other either through personal introductions or name cards;
- a review of the entire agenda; of the expected course of the conference; and of the ground rules, if any;

- a statement of the hoped-for closing time for the session (planning meetings an hour before lunch or quitting time will expedite matters);
- a statement at the beginning of the meeting of any limitations on the group's decision-making or problem-solving powers;
- a periodic summary at logical points in the conference of agreement reached, perhaps even of disagreements;
- assignment of someone to take notes for the record;
- later distribution of the record to the conferees, with any agreements reached.

6. **Evaluation:** It is only natural that one has a desire to know just what progress he or she is making as a conference leader. To satisfy this desire, a conference leadership checklist (Figure 19-1) has been prepared whereby an efficient evaluation of a leader's performance can be made. An inevitable question is that of who evaluates the leader's performance. Because the leader is too busy with the details of leadership it is impossible for the leader to observe his or her own performance in detail. It becomes necessary, therefore, that the service of a conference critic be utilized. But conference critics must be made, just as conference leaders are made. It is commonly accepted, however, that the good leader and good critic can be one and the same individual, performing in one instance as a leader and, in another as a critic. The checklist then has a two-fold purpose: (a) to evaluate the leader's performance and (b) to train the conference critic.

Evaluation Sheet

Conference _____ Date _____

Topic _____ Evaluated by _____

Place a check ( ) in the blank space opposite each point in which you feel the leader appeared to be definitely lax or in which he or she revealed a weakness. (While more than one weakness may be indicated in a statement, the presence of any one in the leader's work is reason enough for checking that statement.)

A. The Introduction
1. Inadequate introduction to topic; group did not understand.   1._____
2. Lecture type of introduction too long, stilted, biased.   2._____
3. Conference not made aware of a real problem to be solved.   3._____

Evaluation Sheet

B. The Leader

4. Leader nervous, erratic, or ill-at-ease. 4._____
5. Referred too much to notes or manual. 5._____
6. Apparently ignorant of topic; unprepared, no planning. 6._____
7. Lectured or expressed own opinions too much. 7._____
8. Lacked zest, enthusiasm and humor. 8._____
9. Slow to grasp and develop pertinent points offered. 9._____
10. Vocabulary inadequate for group. 10._____
11. Boresome over-use of pet phrases. 11._____
12. Too talkative (wordy, not condensed). 12._____
13. Poor tone or modulation of voice. 13._____
14. Kept group too long after closing time. 14._____
15. Abrupt or tactless in handling individuals. 15._____
16. Did not announce next meeting and topic. 16._____

C. The Conference

17. Discussion not well distributed, monopolized by a few. 17._____
18. Failed to arouse and/or sustain lively interest in topic. 18._____
19. Failed to establish and clarify purpose of successive charts. 19._____
20. Side-tracking and lack of attention not energetically checked. 20._____
21. Permitted too much wrangling over words. 21._____
22. Dangerous topics or offensive argument permitted to run. 22._____
23. Too many lags in the discussion. 23._____
24. Not much thought indicated by group in responses, a tendency to agree with others. 24._____
25. Shortage of pertinent and interesting case material. 25._____
26. Failed to clarify and analyze points or cases developed. 26._____
27. Numerous questions left unanswered. 27._____
28. Deviated too far from standard outline. 28._____
29. Poorly framed questions not designed for timely answers. 29._____
30. Poor distribution of time among various phases of topic. 30._____
31. Not enough ground covered in available time. 31._____
32. Failed to draw conclusions and drive them home in closing. 32._____
33. Failed to place charted points before group for approval. 33._____
34. Did not secure understanding of important terms. 34._____

Evaluation Sheet

D. The Charts
35. Charts and spacing poorly planned and organized. 35._____
36. Lettering not legible enough. 36._____
37. Entries too long. 37._____
38. Work too slow. 38._____
39. Entries not sufficiently clear or precise. 39._____
40. Abrupt or awkward transitions from one chart to another. 40._____
41. Not headed in advance. 41._____

E. The Room Conditions
42. Laxity in controlling seating arrangement and interruptions. 42._____
43. Started late without good reason. 43._____
44. Topic title not displayed. 44._____
45. Inadequate chart (as mentioned under "D" above) facilities. 45._____
46. Poor lighting. 46._____

Figure 19-1

The Efficiency of Various Small Group Forms

While we've been concerned up to now with the conference, mainly because it is the most common form of small group, there is more to small group communication. The form of communication will follow the way in which the group is organized by the leader. Professor Alex Bavelas of Massachusetts Institute of Technology performed some pioneering experiments on the effect of various structures of small groups upon their communication efficiency and the morale of the group. The details aren't important here; the experiments were done under laboratory conditions using naval cadets as subjects; and the problem being solved was that of finding a common color in a group of six marbles. The important point relates to the ways in which small groups can be arranged to permit flow of communication by the leader. Each form has a different kind of effect.

1. **The leader as the center.** The first organization form is one which we find in groups where the leader contacts each person individually, and each has little cross-communication with the others. This means that A, B, C and D can all communicate with the leader, and he or she can communicate with them. It also means that they are dependent upon the leader for their information about what is going on elsewhere in the organization, what the objectives of the group might be, and practically any other kind of news about what's happening. This, of course, puts considerable authority in the hands of the leader, since his or her communication system is itself a kind of power. Here are some of the effects

this kind of group has upon group performance and efficiency:
- The centralized group is the most efficient for getting the job done as long as the group is doing routine, repetitive work, such as on a production line.
- If the job is constantly changing, and cross-information is important to adapting to the changes, the centralized group is the least efficient.
- The group members will tend to dislike the part they play in the centralized group and will want to get out of it. The leader, however, always enjoys his or her role in this type of group and thinks it is just great. If this relationship continues, the group may slow down; or, even more likely, the members will quit when they can do so.
- When you have a production routine job to do, line your followers up this way but try to overcome the natural distaste they feel for their role in such a group.

2. **The shared information group.** The second organization form is one in which each member of the group has equally good access to all other members of the group and to the leader. The leader doesn't have any special leverage over the members because of his or her position in the communication system. Here's how the experiments showed this group would behave:
- In production work it would be very inefficient but the members would enjoy the part they played.
- When the job to be done was a constantly changing one, it would still be pretty slow and inefficient but would be more efficient than the first type which often broke down when confronted with changes.
- Even when the problem was changing, the members of the group would be happy about their roles.

3. **The divided lines of authority group.** The third form of group is actually a mixture of the two listed previously. An example of this is the general manager who has production people in the plant and sales people in the field who seldom, if ever, get together. Thus this form of organization might involve having two lines of subordinates who work apart from each other for a single leader. The leader in this type of organization is the focal point of communication. What effect does this have upon performance?
- The leader enjoys his or her role in the group, and the people who report to the leader enjoy their roles fairly well but somewhat less. The people at the bottom enjoy their roles not at all and would like to quit. Often they aren't even certain who the real leader is.
- In terms of efficiency it falls midway between the

first two. It isn't as efficient on production problems as the first group, nor as efficient on changing problems as the second.
- The morale of the people ranges over a wider scale than either of the others.

Chapter 20
Being Effective Before a Crowd

Success will bring with it the occasion to speak in public before live audiences and to give TV interviews to present yourself and your ideas to large groups of people. While it would be patent nonsense to suggest that reading a single chapter will get you ready for that experience, it is possible to start now a program that will prepare for those occasions. All of the fine skills that could be most helpful will come most easily only after considerable practice, yet it is worthwhile to note some of the more important ones which have been gleaned from books and articles, and from research in the leadership of large groups.

This chapter isn't just about public speaking, but all kinds of leadership and persuasion of large groups.

There are several different ways in which you can be placed in a position where large group leadership is important to your success.
- You might be elected to office in a large organization and have to get results through a large number of people.
- You might have to make a speech or chair a large group meeting such as a convention or a civic group.
- You might have to make a presentation or interview on TV where your audience contact is impossible, but where thousands or even millions of people may be watching and hearing you.

In such situations you must follow these three guides to being effective before large audiences:

      1. Be overprepared.
      2. Use tested platform techniques.
      3. Evaluate your accomplishment.

Guides to Knowing What You Are Getting Into

Here are seven basic guides to help you prepare to make that important speech to a large audience:

1. **Be sure the program chairperson has written you a letter.** Don't even show up unless you have a written statement from the program chairperson inviting you and telling you a lot of facts about the meeting in addition to the basics of time and place.

2. **Get a statement of the program chairperson's objectives.** You should not only have a written note telling you what the program chairperson wants you to accomplish, but a specific list of examples of what would be the effect if you were successful. Without such a clear fix you lower your chances of making a suitable presentation. Repeat that set of objectives back in your note of acknowledgement. Unless you are an experienced old pro, never accept a substitute or ad-lib assignment.

3. **Make sure you know the nature and size of the group.** One time when I was young I accepted a speech date over the phone to "give a talk to a seminar for the Grange." When I got there I learned it was the state convention, that I was the keynote speaker, that there were twenty-five hundred women in the audience, and that I was to speak

for the whole morning. My visions of a half-hour talk to twenty or thirty people went flying. Get information about the size, typical titles or jobs, educational level, and so on. If the chairperson has a list of the people's names and occupations or business addresses get that too.

4. **Find out who else or what else the program contains.** You may be surprised to learn that you are the last speaker, following four other people talking on your same subject who have effectively stolen all of your carefully prepared materials. If you see several speakers lined up, send them an outline of your talk and ask them to do the same in return. If you are first on the program, you might be able to set a tone and to keynote what is to follow. If you are last, you can help summarize.

5. **Plan your talk, write it down, then don't read it.** This means getting things ready in advance to master your talk, making notes and practicing your delivery in a room similar in size to the actual presentation room. If they want a text, provide one copy and let them reproduce it but don't hand it out in advance of the meeting. Everyone will be reading along with your talk and trying to catch you in a mistake. Focus the meeting on relating to the group.

6. **Be sure your visual aids are large enough and can be read by everyone.** Generally if you have charts or graphs that are too small you will lose your audience. Letters should be three to four inches tall on the final pojection if they are going to be seen in a large audience. The larger the room, the larger the figures and letters must be. Making their aids a handicap is a common error for first-time speakers.

7. **Give your requirements for audio and visual equipment in advance.** Don't walk into the meeting and announce, "Oh, by the way, I will want a lapel mike rather than a podium mike." It might not be available and your presentation will be crippled when you are forced to stay behind the podium instead of moving about as you'd planned.

Guides to Reaching Your Audience

Here are eleven guides that will help you to reach and hold an audience:

1. **Show up early to visit the room where the meeting is going to occur.** Don't get trapped in a reception, dinner or party before you speak that will result in your seeing the room for the first time when you walk on stage to be introduced.

2. **Practice your visual aids to be sure they work right and are of the right size and clarity, and to be sure that the equipment you require is all present and working.** Always use a mike if the room is large or the crowd is large. You have an obligation to make sure that you can be heard. You shouldn't have to ask a nervous "Can you all hear me in the rear of the room?" before you start. You should know that because you got there and tested the sound level in advance.

3. **Start off your talk with an attention getter.** A former dean at Harvard used to catch the attention of his freshman audience by saying, "Look to your left, now look to your right. One of you won't be here by the end of the first semester." This assured him that they were all listening. Such statements would also fit a business audience since one business in three will fail this year. The best attention getter talks directly

to the audience being addressed with something that is important to them or that could be made important to them.

4. **Don't use humor or jokes unless you are very good at it.** One of the most painful experiences for speakers is to tell a joke that goes flat. It's better to rely upon facts, information or sincere interest. Never use puns. Wry humor, or jokes that are droll, often go better and can be slipped in between your main points.

5. **Pick a few major points and hammer them hard.** Don't try to cover everything in every detail in a single speech. Outline five, six or seven major points you would like to make and emphasize them. Tell them first what you are going to tell them. ("Tonight I am going to tell you why this town can't afford to continue with an inferior school system. I have ten arguments, which I am now going to list, and then will prove each in turn.") Then, as you cover each point, tell them where you are. (Let's look at point five.") Summarize your talk at the end. Tell them what you have told 'em, and quit.

6. **Look at your audience, using the baseball diamond system.** When you are standing in front of an audience, imagine that you are a catcher on a baseball team. As you talk move your eyes to catch those of the first baseman, the pitcher, the second baseman, then back to first, over to third, and take an occasional glance into left and right field. Then look at the bench. Skip around. Look at one person at a time in this way and talk to each personally. The impression will be for every person in the audience that you are looking at them personally. Keep your eyes going from base to base, player to player. Never fix on your notes, or on the ceiling, or on the podium.

7. **Use lots of examples, cases and illustrations to make your points.** "For-instances" are more easily remembered and can dramatize your point better than raw facts, and most especially better than raw emotional assertions of your case. Facts and statistics should be used like salt–in small amounts they can add flavor and taste to what you are saying. Large tables and lengthy recitations of figures leave the audience in a stupor. Let people see the human effects of your point through examples, for it's easier to identify with people like oneself than with numbers or ideas.

8. **Show why your ideas are important now.** Don't get too deeply into the history of your argument or give a lot of "background" information. Show why you are bringing the subject up now and what the consequences will be in the immediate future if your present warning isn't heeded. ("If we allow this new mall to be built, thirty cents out of every dollar you now bring into your business will disappear within one month.")

9. **Ask for some action at the end of your presentation.** Tell people the answer to their implied question: "So what?" make your program a three-point plan, or a five-point plan. Don't be overly general leaving them with some dangling verbalizations such as "and if we don't all change our ways America is doomed." However true that may be, it doesn't ask for the order or suggest a specific change which your audience can act upon right then. A better close would go like this: "Ladies and gentlemen, I think all of this adds up to a four-point plan

which everyone in this room can start working on tonight. First. . ." Then ask them to do something.

10. **Don't overestimate people's information nor underestimate their intelligence.** Bad speakers often assume that their problem and all the facts are well known to the audience, and that the audience is very well informed about the issue. They should, instead, assume that technical words and special jargon are not understood and should thus use ordinary language. Don't presume that everyone knows all about "the infamous Burlington Mall case." Tell them about it if you are going to base your suggestions on that evidence.

11. **Use the rules of persuasion if you are trying to persuade people to do something.** The cardinal rule of persuasion is "Appear to be balanced." You give all of the arguments in favor of your case, then balance it off by presenting all of the negative arguments for the opposition. A second important rule of persuasion is to "Cite the features of your case and the benefits of each feature." For example, in speaking about a downtown rebuilding program you might zero in on better storefronts, a stronger merchant organization, and more effective promotional campaigns. Then cite the benefits of each. ("The better storefronts will get you more dollar sales through repeat business and more traffic in your store.") A third rule of persuasion is to "List the possible options." You then proceed to knock out all of those except the one you are trying to sell to your audience. Emphasize how easy it is to get started and how simple your action plan is. Then ask them to start on the first step.

Follow-Up and Evaluation

If you have made a speech, no matter how well or poorly you think you have done, always try to get some feedback from the audience or from the program chairperson about how well it worked. Don't simply ask, "Did you like my talk?" Instead ask, "What did you like best and what did you like least?" Listen most carefully to the responses, especially the latter. You can improve if you face the facts about how well you did the first time. If time and circumstances permit, you can get a very accurate measurement by passing out questionnaires asking for reactions. Always seek out copies of the actual responses if they are available and read the critical comments most carefully.

You might turn into a great speaker, which is a useful skill in gaining personal effectiveness, and you'll enjoy it immensely.

Chapter 21
Planning Follow-Up Development

Somebody asked a college president how it was that colleges could accumulate so much knowledge. "I suspect that it is because the freshmen bring so much, and the seniors take so little away when they leave," he answered. This book inevitably leaves the writer feeling the same way. There is so much more than should be covered, but the pressures of time and the economics of publishing mean that everything cannot be covered.

Since this book clearly isn't a scholarly tome but is a teaching bok aimed at changing your behavior to increase your personal effectiveness, it would be a shame just to drop everything here. Learning isn't something you do once and then quit doing. It is a lifelong process. The best result of reading a book is not to set the finished book aside, satisfied, but to ask, "What should I read next?" Such is the purpose of this concluding chapter.

The Art of Plain Talk by Rudolf Flesch (Harper & Row, 1946).

"This is a book on plain talk. It tells you how to speak and write so that people understand what you mean." This is the beginning of the 210-page book which demonstrates that the author knows his stuff. He writes in plain talk, and you can understand him. This doesn't mean he is a simple-minded dolt. He has reseach evidence galore which shows convincingly that he is right. This book is a good starter both for beginners and advanced speakers and writers. People who have been trained to produce gobbledygook should be forced by law to read and apply this book.

The Elements of Style by William Strunk, Jr. and E.B. White (Macmillan, 2nd Edition 1972).

If you'd like a little (71-page) book that will make your writing clean and correct, you should get this book, study it and keep it at your right hand. This little guide to style in writing was written by a professor at Cornell University. Many famous writers, including E.B. White, studied under Strunk and became sound technicians of writing usage and style. The book barks orders about grammar like a drill instructor. "Choose a suitable design and hold to it," for example, gives you no-nonsense advice on writing. The last chapter has twenty-one reminders for good writing. As White puts it: "Get the **little** book. Get the **little** book. Get the **little** book." Okay, so go **get** it. Otherwise you may waste a lifetime learning to write well.

The American Language by H.L. Mencken (Alfred A. Knopf, 3 volumes, 4th Edition 1946).

If the above has whetted your appetite and you want to move into the big leagues, or are confined to bed for a month, try this really great book. Originally published in 1919 by a famous columnist and newspaperman, it is immensely readable and informative. This book deals with all of the words that make up the American Language; how the language developed from its various foreign origins; how slang emerged, and its impact on our times. After reading it you'll be convinced that language is a beautiful thing, and that words are bullets, songs, and winged creatures.

Are You Listening by Ralph Nichols and L.A. Stevens (McGraw-Hill, 1957).

If listening is your interest, the best book is clearly this widely-read and readable one by Nichols and Stevens. Although most of us spend a high percentage of our time listening, we don't really retain more than twenty-five percent of what we hear. This practical work gives you some tested methods for improving your own listening and retaining ability. The common errors that prevent us from really hearing are spelled out; and their cures, as well.

How to Cash in on Your Hidden Memory Power by William D. Hersey (Prentice-Hall, 1963).

If you find that you have trouble remembering things and want some detailed methods for improving your memory, here's a most readable and comprehensive "how-to" book. This work focuses on changing you from a person with an ordinary memory to one with what the author calls a "thinking machine mind." Drawing on the basic principles, he also weaves in some newer concepts from computer technology, without getting esoteric about it. He deals with remembering numbers, financial statements, catalogues, stock prices, names, faces and groups. He then goes on to tell you how to cash in on this enlarged skill. You can be more successful, make more profit, and be a hero to your kids.

How to Win Friends and Influence People by Dale Carnegie (Simon & Schuster, 1936).

This is the classic in the human relations field which everyone should read. Millions of copies have been printed and read in almost every language on earth. It started the human relations movement which has grown to tremendous proportions. Although some of its techniques and illustrations are now considered slightly old-fashioned and dated by modern behavioral sciences standards, there remains a hard core of experience-proved ideas for every success-minded person who works with other people.

Reading Skills by William D. Baker (Prentice-Hall, 2nd Edition 1974).
How to Read Faster and Better by Norman Lewis (Thomas Y. Crowell, 4th Edition 1978).

If your reading speed is under two hundred and fifty words a minute and your comprehension less than eighty percent, you may be a prime candidate for one of these works. Both teach you how to read faster–say, up to eight hundred or a thousand words per minute with serious practice, without loss of understanding. Either of them will do fine.

The Human Side of Enterprise by Douglas McGregor (McGraw-Hill, 1960).

This work deals with Theory X and Theory Y, as well as with some other practical aspects of human relations in supervision and management, such as training, performance appraisal, and compensation.

Managerial Psychology by Harold J. Leavitt (University of Chicago Press, 4th Edition 1978).

This is a college text, but it's certainly much more readable and understandable than most. It's also comprehensive. Starting with individuals, the book moves up to small groups and finally to organizations, showing them as related to one another. Relevant psychological facts are here, plus the research evidence behind them. It's easy reading, too.

Games People Play; The Psychology of Human Relationships by Eric Berne (Grove Press, 1964).

This is, without doubt, a readable and quotable book from the best-seller lists that you can put into immediate action, even if only in small group conversation. Doctor Berne, a serious practitioner and psychiatrist, has written a fascinating book on how people relate to one another in what he calls "games". It's written in common parlance and loaded with illustrations for each principle. All of us, he says, have three ego states—Parent, Adult and Child. The way in which we relate to others depends upon our state and theirs. The game consists of finding the right kind of transaction.

Motivation and Personality by Abraham H. Maslow, editor (Harper & Row, 2nd Edition 1970).

The major contribution of this book is the clear spelling out of the idea of a hierachy of motives. It deals with those **inner** causes of **outward** behavior.

The Image: Knowledge in Life and Society by Kenneth Boulding (University of Michigan Press, 1956).

This is a clear statement of how images affect behavior. It suggests that the image lies behind the action of every individual, and that it is the key to most knowledge.

A Dynamic Theory of Personality by Kurt Lewin (McGraw-Hill, 1935).

Somewhat tougher reading, more scientifically oriented, is a text which deals with "field forces" and managing the situation. The works of the pioneer in the field of group dynamics are presented here in eight papers. They deal with the psychology of the individual and his or her environment. Much of this is about child psychology, but there's also something here for you and your personality and your environment.

The Analysis of Behavior by James Holland and B.F. Skinner (McGraw-Hill, 1961).

Unfortunately, you'll really have to dig in for further reading in learning theory and behavioral technology because practically everything written in the field is in technical language. This is the best work for general readers and it's really a simple book in many ways since it is a programmed instruction text. Written by two professors from Harvard, the latter being the father of the teaching machine, it is a self-instruction manual. You'll have to learn the content in order to finish the text. If you really would like to take a self-taught course in behavior, this is it.

MBO II: A System of Managerial Leadership for the 80's by George S. Odiorne (Pitman, 1979).

The systems approach is described in greater detail in this book by the present author. This book deals with a system of leadership in which the first step calls for defining objectives in terms of specific results expected. This is an updated version of the author's original 1965 book on Management by Objectives.

Work Simplification: Creative Thinking About Work Problems by Robert Lehrer (Prentice-Hall, 1957).

This is a detailed outline of major and specific minor points in simplifying activities in manufacturing and elsewhere by a professor if industrial engineering at Georgia Tech.

There are, of course, countless other books which would fit into this list and from which the materials in this book are drawn. The list above comprises what seems to this author to be a basic list. You might be surprised to know that although many of these books are twenty to forty years old, each is still in print at the time this book was written and many are available in inexpensive paperback editions. Why not pick the most interesting and get started?